how to meditate

hamlyn
how to meditate
Paul Roland

Executive Editor: Jane McIntosh
Senior Editor: Trevor Davies
Editor: Mary Lambert
Creative Director: Keith Martin
Executive Art Editor: Mark Winwood
Design: Rozelle Bentheim
Illustration: Glen Wilkins
Picture Research: Christine Jünemann
Production Controller: Lucy Woodhead

First published in Great Britain in 2000
by Hamlyn, an imprint of
Octopus Publishing Group Limited,
2–4 Heron Quays, London E14 4JP

Copyright © 2000 Octopus Publishing Group Limited

ISBN 0 600 59914 0

A catalogue record for this book is available from the British Library

Produced by Toppan
Printed in China

introduction
the benefits of meditation

I have been practising, teaching and writing about meditation for more than 20 years and it is no exaggeration to say that it has changed my life, and the lives of my students, in a profoundly positive way. I believe that it can do the same for everyone who learns the basic skills. With that aim in mind I have collated a number of different exercises for this book that I have found to be particularly effective, so that you can discover the value of meditation for yourself.

Although meditation is often associated with an ascetic, spiritual lifestyle there is no need for anyone to renounce their own beliefs or neglect their everyday obligations in order to practise it, or to reap the benefits. Whatever technique you adopt, you can find your 'true self' in the serenity of meditation.

'If there is no meditation then you are like a
blind man in a world of great beauty, light
and colour.' (Krishnamurti)

a personal view

My first experience of meditation came when I attended a yoga class which the other students and I expected would concentrate on the familiar physical postures. But during the relaxation period at the end of the first lesson the teacher took us through a simple guided visualization during which we were to imagine ourselves up in the night sky floating free of our physical bodies.

It might sound improbable, but focusing in this way while being completely relaxed had an extraordinary effect on me, and I experienced what can only be described as an expansion of consciousness. My mind felt as if it had become detached from my body and in those few timeless moments this sense of detachment brought a profound sense of serenity. I felt no physical sensations at all. It seemed as if my mind was filling the room and that I was pure consciousness.

This was the 'real' me, not the name or the person that I presented to the outside world. It was not what I would now consider to be a mystical experience, but neither was it simply just a new form of relaxation. It was more like a waking dream in which I was at peace, but at the same time still in control and entirely aware of my surroundings.

MEDITATING REGULARLY

After the yoga class I started meditating for ten minutes every day because it offered an opportunity to experience such altered states of consciousness while remaining fully in control. In time I lost my fear of the unknown, which, incidentally, is one of the many secondary benefits of meditation, and I developed a more positive outlook on life in general.

Meditation became pleasantly addictive. The more regularly I practised the more benefits I gained and the longer the effects lasted. Over time I attended a number of meditation courses and eventually taught classes and workshops of my own. The students shared similar experiences to mine and derived the same benefits, so that when the courses ended there was always a demand to continue in their own time at another venue.

'The gift of learning to meditate is the greatest gift you can give yourself in this life.'

(Sogyal Rinpoche)

Right: For Buddhists meditation is not a practice but a state of mind. Buddhists put great emphasis on the benefits of relaxing from the 'anxious self'.

'There is no need for temples; no need for complicated philosophy. Our own brain, our own heart is our temple; my philosophy is kindness.' (The Dalai Lama)

Everyone who I shared a class with, or whom I later taught, benefited in some way from practising meditation. One lady came to one of my classes because she felt drained of energy every evening after having cared for her sick husband all day. She took up meditation on a daily basis and soon felt revitalized, positive and more able to cope. Another lady used a simple visualization technique to find relief from severe migraine headaches, again finding success on the first try.

I also taught a group of severely stressed employees at a multi-national pharmaceutical company who habitually had their sleep disturbed by worries concerning their work. Once awake they were unable to get back to sleep, and became increasingly tired and depressed. After adopting a simple visualization routine, which I urged them to practise just before going to sleep each night, they were able to get their first uninterrupted night's sleep in months. In addition, they found that they were also able to concentrate more effectively on their work during the day.

WHY MEDITATE?

People come to meditation for various reasons and with different expectations. Initially, it is enough to approach your meditation practice as just another element of your daily exercise routine and take from it whatever you need, be it relief from stress, improved physical and mental health or a sustained sense of wellbeing. In time, as your awareness increases, you may feel the urge to explore altered states of consciousness in search of the answers to the questions that fascinate us all. If, and when, you are ready to do so, you will find a number of original exercises in the final sections of this book that will guide you safely to discover what is true for you.

how meditation affects the body

Above: **By adopting a balanced and relaxed posture we can attain a state of serenity and heightened awareness.**

It is now generally accepted that the mind can influence the mechanical body functions and the chemical balance which ensures good health. When the mind is disturbed or conditioned to think in a negative way it can cause an imbalance in the body which we call dis-ease (old spelling derived from French, *desaise*). Worry, anxiety and resentment can also restrict the free flow of vital energy which will then show up as physical symptoms unless the balance is restored. Again, meditation has been proven to be highly effective in treating the source of these disturbances in the psyche which are immune to conventional drug treatment.

BALANCING THE BODY

In clinical tests meditation has been found to be highly effective both as a complementary therapy or when used to support orthodox medical treatment. It helps to balance the right and left hemispheres of the brain which relate to the emotional and intellectual processes respectively, and strengthens the immune system so that the body can heal itself.

Meditation's considerable biological benefits include regulating blood pressure, stimulating blood circulation, alleviating pain and reducing muscular tension. It can even slow down hormonal activity, so that people who practise meditation on a regular basis begin to look healthier and feel fitter.

Minor ailments such as migraine, anxiety attacks, sinus problems, asthma and cardiac arrhythmias can also be helped by regular deep-breathing exercises which improve the circulation of air through constricted passages. For these reasons an increasing number of doctors are beginning to refer patients with stress-related ailments and even terminal illnesses to meditation classes.

But even if you feel physically fit and healthy there are considerable benefits to be gained from integrating meditation into your daily routine. By practising it regularly you can develop self-discipline, improve your personal performance in sports, business and the arts, build self-confidence, increase your energy and efficiency, and generally create a more positive attitude to life.

THE DIFFERENT PHYSIOLOGICAL EFFECTS

According to a series of scientific experiments carried out in the 1960s by Robert Wallace of the University of California in the USA, and subsequently confirmed by Harvard cardiologist, Herbert Benson, meditation has a more profound physiological effect on the body than merely relaxing or even sleeping. Wallace and Benson discovered subjects in a meditative state inhaled 20 per cent less oxygen and exhaled 20 per cent less carbon dioxide than they would do when relaxing in the conventional manner. Their blood pressure and heart rates also fell significantly and they produced significantly less lactic acid which remained at a low level for some time after the sessions had ended. Lactic acid is a substance linked with the fight-or-flight response, and is therefore traditionally used as an indicator of stress levels.

FURTHER RESEARCH

Later in the 1960s, research by two Japanese researchers revealed that during meditation the brain waves of Zen monks exhibited the pattern corresponding to the low Theta frequency usually associated with sleep, although the monks were wide awake and in a heightened state of awareness.

The subsequent discovery that meditation can be used to control the involuntary physiological functions, such as the heart rate and body temperature, led to the development of biofeedback in the 1970s, an alternative technique during which patients mimic meditation techniques for pain and stress relief.

But in addition to the proven psycho-biological benefits meditation can be the first step on the path to self-discovery and greater awareness leading ultimately to Enlightenment, where we attain a state of detachment which the Buddhists describe as being 'in the world but not of it'.

'[Meditation] opens the mind of man to the greatest mystery that takes place daily and hourly; it widens the heart so that it may feel the eternity of time and the infinity of space in every throb; it gives us a life within the world as if we were moving about in paradise and all these spiritual deeds take place without any refuge to doctrine, but by the simple and direct holding fast to the truth which dwells in our innermost being.' (D.T. Suzuki)

the inner self

'Meditation does not come easily. A beautiful tree grows slowly. One must wait for the blossom, the ripening of the fruit and the ultimate taste. The blossom of meditation is an inexpressible peace that permeates the entire being. Its fruit...is indescribable.'

(Swami Vishnu Devananda)

It is only comparatively recently that people in the West have become acutely aware of the importance of nutrition and exercise in maintaining physical health. But we continue to take our mental health and emotional wellbeing for granted, for which we may pay dearly in the future with all manner of psychosomatic symptoms and stress-related disorders.

Western culture is founded on the relentless quest for ever greater material gain and personal comfort. It tends to measure achievement in technological advances and to see fulfilment in terms of social, economic and professional status. In such a climate little regard is given to the needs of the psyche or the soul, for spirituality has long been confused with religious dogma, but if our inner needs are neglected then no matter how successful we may become we are more than likely to come to a crisis at some point in our adult life when possessions, professional achievements and social status lose their appeal. At such times of uncertainty we can be left wondering if life has any real significance and, if so, what the purpose of ours might be.

Where once we might have put our faith in orthodox religion we may now instead be drawn to one of the many 'alternative' beliefs in our search for answers. But belief systems are largely speculative and mystical experiences are personal and subjective. No one has all the answers we seek, nor is there any way in which we can delegate our own spiritual development to someone else, just as we cannot get someone to exercise on our behalf so that we can become physically fit. Ultimately, each person must look within themselves for the answers they seek.

BECOMING SELF-AWARE

As Lao Tzu, the great Chinese philosopher and founder of Taoism remarked, 'the thousand-mile journey begins with one step', and on the long journey towards self-awareness meditation provides that first significant step. It provides us with a quiet time for ourselves, time to discover who we really are and what we want from life. Practised twice daily (morning and evening) for as little as ten minutes at a time it offers the opportunity for each

of us to create what is effectively a sacred space in which to nurture a sense of wellbeing, tap our inner resources and find lasting peace of mind.

It is a common fallacy that meditation is only for people who are 'spiritually advanced'. Anyone can meditate if they put their mind to it. As with any activity that requires a degree of self-discipline it becomes easier with practice and pleasantly addictive, once you begin to feel the benefits.

FOCUSING THE MIND

We all meditate in one form or another whenever we lose ourselves in a routine task, in music or a film, for example, or when we are transfixed by the beauty of nature. However, such moments are rare and fleeting. Through passive contemplation or active concentration, meditation can harness this capacity for detachment at will so that we can learn to still our scattered thoughts and focus our mind.

In this heightened state of awareness the body is relaxed and we are no longer self- or ego-centred but centred within our 'true nature'. Having attained this blissful state, there is then the opportunity to use meditation for examining the psyche. This includes exploring the unconscious and experiencing the inner and external dimensions of the spirit from which we can derive insights, guidance and a profound understanding of the nature of existence and the part that we have chosen to play in its unfolding.

Left: The Chinese Philosopher and founder of Taoism Lâo Tzu who once said 'abide at the centre of your being for the more you leave it, the less you learn'.

IMPORTANT SAFETY NOTE

Meditation is perfectly safe unless you have recently experienced mental or emotional problems, or are taking either prescribed or illegal drugs. Those who are nervous of encountering psychic phenomena or are worried about triggering involuntary out-of-body experiences should first concentrate on the grounding exercises which are designed to calm and balance the mind (see pages 50–51). Meditation is not concerned with such phenomena which, incidentally, can occur to anybody at any time. In such cases meditation may prove beneficial in helping to channel an over-active imagination to a more positive purpose.

why meditate?

It is a common misconception that meditation and conventional forms of relaxation are the same thing. However, meditation is not the passive act that it appears, and when practised regularly it has the potential to bring far greater benefits than simple relaxation.

While relaxation offers temporary relief from stress, meditation aims to achieve both relaxation of the body and a heightened state of awareness. Regular meditation can bring greater control over restless thoughts and emotions leading to a sense of wellbeing.

The practice of meditation has a cumulative affect and the benefits can be felt almost immediately – a sense of detachment from the pressures of life and lasting peace of mind.

1

the many paths to enlightenment

'Know thyself.' (Anonymous inscription on the Temple

of Apollo at Delphi)

In the West we are still preoccupied with the need to explain the mechanics and mysteries of the mind, whereas in the East the aim is to transcend it.

For that reason many Westerners are puzzled and perhaps even put off taking up meditation by talk of 'surrendering to the Higher Self', of 'emptying the mind' and of 'meditating on nothingness' in an effort to discover one's 'true nature'. Such terms might strike some as abstract or irrational, but the meditative state of relaxed awareness is a state to which we all ought to aspire for the sake of our spiritual, mental, emotional and physical wellbeing. As previously stated, it is not necessary to subscribe to any particular belief system or philosophy to practise meditation. However, to deny the spiritual tradition from which it evolved would be to limit its potential for personal transformation before the journey had even begun.

INNER DEPTHS

There is now an acceptance among both the medical establishment and the general public that meditation has psychological benefits, but many are reluctant to see it as more than just another complementary therapy. They can not imagine how sitting in quiet contemplation can bring greater understanding of the world, for they have been conditioned to equate understanding with the accumulation of knowledge and they believe that both come from intense and prolonged study, while wisdom only comes with experience. However, according to Eastern philosophy and the Western esoteric tradition, the source of wisdom and inspiration is within. Whether we call this wisdom the 'Higher Self', the Soul, our Buddha nature or the Christ Consciousness, it is both the immortal essence of our being and an indivisible element of the 'Universal Mind'.

One of the aims of meditation is to subdue the restless chattering of the ego (the conscious mind) and train it to submit to the 'Higher Self' so that we can achieve an expansion of consciousness at will. When we attain this altered state we experience supreme understanding and the bliss of true peace which is known as Enlightenment.

Contrary to popular belief Enlightenment is not limited to ascetics, saints or mystics. It is within the grasp of everyone to manifest their 'true nature' within their lifetime for we are, in essence, Divine. It is just that we are living in denial. As the Indian avatar Sai Baba says, 'I am God; you too are God. The only difference is that I know it and you do not.' Meditation offers us the means by which we can heighten our sensitivity to the still, small voice within and transcend our physical perception to glimpse the 'Greater Reality' that is beyond. Various traditions have developed different techniques for achieving this.

THE BUDDHIST RELIGION

Buddhism makes no distinction between sacred and secular life; every act is performed as if it is the subject of meditation. In Buddhism, as in many other traditions, meditation is not seen as something to be mastered, but as a state of mind that we can slip into in the same way that we relax when our daily work is done.

Sogyal Rinpoche, a modern Buddhist master and author of *The Tibetan Book of Living and Dying*, suggests that meditation is simply the art of letting go: 'In meditation, be at ease, be as natural and spacious as possible. Slip quietly out of the noose of your habitual anxious self and relax into your 'true nature'.'

Above: The simplicity of a Zen garden is designed to still the mind rather than engage it.

Once we find peace of mind we are not to try to possess it, but rather to remain in a state of 'calm abiding'. When thoughts arise they should be considered as transient and insignificant as ripples on the surface of a lake which will return to tranquillity. In this serene state negativity, aggression and confusion simply cannot exist.

ZEN BUDDHISM

In the form of Zen Buddhism known as Rinzai, teachers lead their pupils towards enlightenment by confounding their rational minds with an enigmatic form of riddle known as a *koan* so that the inner chatter is silenced and intuition takes over. A typical exchange was that which took place between the Indian sage Boddhidharma and a pupil who pleaded with his master to pacify his mind to which the Boddhidharma replied, 'Show me your mind.' When the pupil confessed that it was impossible, his master remarked, 'There, I have pacified your mind.'

Koans are a technique particular to Rinzai which roughly translates as 'sudden'. It describes a direct, confrontational form which is intended to shock the mind into a state in which perceptions and values are rendered meaningless so that the initiate can accept a new reality. In contrast, Soto Zen requires its followers to practise a 'Serene Reflection' method which involves sitting in silence and allowing the mind to settle like silt stirred up in a muddy pond. Once this state has been attained, acute awareness, and ultimately Enlightenment, follow naturally. Zen tends to confound the logical mind because it contradicts the belief that life has a meaning. Instead Zen philosophy says that life is simply a moment of being.

Above: In yoga each posture is considered as meditation in action.

Right: Whichever form of yogic meditation one adopts, the aim is to lose one's sense of separateness and become absorbed in the silence.

HINDU BELIEFS

In the Hindu tradition there are ten distinct limbs of yoga, all leading to Enlightenment. Dhyana yoga is the form concerned with meditation, while Laya yoga seeks to manifest the divine spark by stimulating the chakras, the subtle energy centres situated in the etheric, or spiritual, body. One way in which this can be done is to use meditations where the initiate visualizes these vortices as blossoming lotus flowers of varying colours (see page 60). Dhyana yoga has two approaches. The first is called Saguna, and here the mind is focused on an object, mantra (sacred words for concentration) or symbol, to the extent that all sense of the physical reality is rendered meaningless. In the second, Nirguna, the subject of the meditation is abstract and in this the initiate seeks total absorption. Either approach sees yoga as a form of meditation with each of the yoga asanas, or postures, being a form of meditation in action.

THE KABBALAH

At the heart of the Western esoteric tradition is the more intellectual approach embodied in the Kabbalah, the Jewish mystical teachings which state that everything in existence is an expression of its Creator and that every human being is cast in the image of the Absolute. In this scheme humans are seen as the microcosm, or a universe in minature. Therefore to know the mysteries of existence and the nature of the Creator we first have to know ourselves. This self-awareness is to be obtained through study of the allegorical tales of the Old Testament, which tells of the soul's descent into matter and the path we must travel in order to reunite with the 'Source', and from knowledge of a central symbolic glyph known as the Tree of Life. This diagram serves as a map both of the human psyche and of the structure of existence which we can explore and experience through guided meditations known as Pathworking (see page 106).

Practical Kabbalah is thought to be the earliest form of structured meditation. Its roots can be traced to an earlier tradition known as Merkabah (the Work of the Chariot) in which the initiate heightens their awareness of the higher worlds using visualizations. It was a technique which is believed to have been central to the spiritual discipline and practice of the ascetic Jewish sects known as the Essenes and the Nazarenes, of whom Joshua Ben Miriam (Jesus) is believed to have been an initiate.

The Essenes established a community at Qumram, which can today be found in north western Jordan, where the Dead Sea Scrolls were discovered, and it was here that they practised a form of yoga where they sought to

harmonize the seven complementary attributes of the
Earthly Mother and of the Heavenly Father which
corresponded to the chakras (the body's spiritual
centres) in the etheric body.

In practice, this involved meditations on a symbol also
known as the Tree of Life (see page 108) whose seven
branches stretched heavenwards and whose seven roots
reached down into the earth with the human body
representing the trunk which was to be a channel for the
terrestrial and celestial forces.

All of these traditions developed diverse methods of
self-awareness that were essentially variations on a
similar theme. What they emphasized was the knowledge
that meditation is not an end in itself, but the means to
an end in which we are to bring the insights, compassion
and serenity gained in meditation into daily life.

'What really matters is not just the practice of
sitting but far more the state of mind you find
yourself in after meditation. It is this calm and
centred state of mind you should prolong
through everything you do.' (Sogyal Rinpoche)

transcendental meditation

Above: Maharishi Mahesh Yogi, founder
of TM and personal guru to the Beatles.

The increasing popularity of Transcendental Meditation (TM) as an aid to developing greater self-awareness and as a complementary therapy has prompted the medical establishment to subject its techniques and extraordinary claims to intense scientific study. The results of over 500 studies carried out at 214 universities and research institutes worldwide over the past 30 years make a convincing case for the effectiveness of TM and meditation in general as a holistic system of natural healthcare, and as a successful system for stress relief. The conclusion reached by researchers at Stanford University in the USA in the 1980s was particularly persuasive. After comparing 144 methods of relaxation the Stanford team concluded that TM was more than twice as effective as any other relaxation technique.

Although the four million practitioners of TM worldwide make great claims for its psycho-biological benefits, in essence it is no different from any other meditation technique and therefore the claims made for its effectiveness can apply equally to all forms of meditation. It differs from traditional forms of meditation in only one respect; it emphasizes the importance of adopting a personal mantra which is to be kept secret from the other members of the group. This is one reason why TM has been criticised for cultivating a cult-like clique. The other is that it prohibits anyone other than a teacher who has been personally trained by its founder, Maharishi Mahesh Yogi, from teaching the technique.

Since the results of this survey were published more than 100 major Japanese multi-national corporations, including Sony, have implemented TM into their training programmes, and have so far have been impressed with its benefits.

HEALTH GAINS

TM is also gaining widespread acceptance with the medical profession specifically in relation to stress relief, psychosomatic disorders and the treatment of addictions from tobacco to hard drugs.

A recent study published in the international medical journal *Psychosomatic Medicine* revealed that over a five-year period regular TM practitioners required comparatively less medical treatment than the control subjects. The 2,000-strong TM group were found to need 87 per cent fewer hospitalizations for heart disease, 55 per cent fewer for tumours, 87 per cent fewer for nervous disorders and 73 per cent fewer for lung, throat and nose complaints.

The scientific evidence was so persuasive that in 1993 a group of 136 British doctors successfully petitioned the then Secretary of State for Health to make TM available in Britain. Now an increasing number of doctors are taking up the practice themselves (more than 700 according to the British Health Education Authority) having been impressed by the effect it has had on their patients. These impressive statistics have even persuaded various health-insurance companies to offer substantial discounts to policy-holders who practise TM!

BRAIN PATTERNS

Although critics of alternative therapies argue that the meditators' claims of achieving altered states of consciousness are all in the mind, it would appear that meditation has a physical effect on the brain that can be mapped and measured. According to Professor N. Lyubimov, one of the world's leading neuroscientists and a director of the Neurocybernetics Laboratory at

TM FOR BUSINESS AND SHOW BUSINESS

TM was introduced to the West in 1958 by Maharishi Mahesh Yogi (who was personal guru to the pop group the Beatles and other 1960s celebrities) and since then it has been adopted by movie stars such as Arnold Schwarzenegger, Sylvester Stallone, Clint Eastwood and Elizabeth Taylor, international sports personalities and high-flying business executives. In 1987 a leading Japanese company, Sumitomo Heavy Industries, introduced TM to 600 of its managers and monitored their progress and productivity over the following 18 months. Sumitomo recorded a considerable drop in absenteeism and a significant increase in individual performance and quality of work. The managers claimed their health had improved and that they suffered less from stress which in turn gave them a a happier home life.

Moscow's Brain Research Institute in Russia, meditation produces a unique pattern of coherent activity in the brain's frontal cortex creating a state of 'restful alertness' and improved mental performance. From these findings Professor Lyubimov predicted that in the future meditation will be utilized 'to tap the vast hidden reserves of the human brain' and map its mysteries.

starting to meditate

'When you meditate there should be no effort to control and no attempt to be peaceful. Do not be overly solemn, or feel that you are taking part in some special ritual. Let go even of the idea that you are meditating. Let your body remain as it is and your breath as you find it.' (Sogyal Rinpoche)

It is a common fallacy that meditation comes more easily to individuals of Eastern extraction. Meditation is the natural state of the mind, but Western culture has made it difficult for Americans and Europeans, in particular, to establish the habit. From early childhood we are constantly bombarded with external stimuli until we become addicted to sensation. We are conditioned to seek constant stimulation and satisfaction of all the senses – whether it be in food, fashion, entertainment, drink or drugs, the ultimate 'quick fix'. We are made to feel self-conscious, anti-social and even eccentric if we express the need to take time out for ourselves to meditate. While yoga has become a fashionable addition to the regular exercise routine, meditation is still generally seen as slightly strange and self-indulgent.

For these reasons Westerners have an inner resistance to meditation, on principle. So this is the first major hurdle that you will need to overcome if you are to meditate regularly.

MAKING TIME TO MEDITATE

Initially you will probably find lots of other things that seem in more urgent need of your attention and you will

Right: It is important to discipline yourself into maintaining an everyday period of relaxation and focusing.

be tempted to put off your meditation time indefinitely. Do not do that. There is no better time to start meditating than the present, so when you have finished reading this sentence shut the book, close your eyes, and take a few

PRACTISING MEDITATION

How did you find it? No doubt it was harder than you thought it would be. Did you find your mind wandering? Did thoughts nag at you reminding you of all those chores you have not done? Did you find it difficult to sit still? Did you want to scratch or fidget? Whatever your experience, take some comfort from the fact that everyone who has meditated has felt something of your frustration when they first began. Like most disciplines, from learning to read to playing a musical instrument, it becomes easier with practice.

minutes to sit in silence.

As for all those things that you feel you ought to be doing instead of meditating, persevere and you will soon find that you readily put off everything else in order to meditate. It is then that you will have to be careful that you do not become hooked on the experience.

In certain respects meditation is no different to physical exercise. Both require a certain amount of self-discipline if the habit is to be established. It is a good idea to meditate at the same time every day, even if it is only for ten minutes, so encourage yourself by making that time

of the day a special time. Create an inviting atmosphere with candles, incense and a small vase of fresh lightly scented flowers (see page 27).

It will also help if you have a specific focus for each session, such as sending healing to people you know who are in need, or to a particular area of the world where people are suffering (see page 58). Absent healing is one of the best ways to cultivate compassion and to stop being so self-centred, which are two essential steps on the path to peace of mind and, ultimately, to Enlightenment.

LEARNING TO RELAX

Another thing that you will need to nurture is the ability to relax. We all assume that relaxation comes naturally to us, but it does not. We have been conditioned to believe that we must constantly be active and productive. A certain amount of stress can be stimulating because it releases adrenaline which is energizing in certain situations, but we can become addicted to that natural chemical 'high'. That is why it is important to establish a balance between mental or physical activity and quiet contemplation.

When we do relax it tends to be in a passive, unfocused way. This is dissimilar from the meditation experience which aims for heightened awareness and total relaxation of the body. I often think of meditation as being similar to swimming, as to be successful at either depends on the ability to relax. If you relax in the water you will find it easier to swim because the water will support you, but if you become tense you will sink.

DIFFERENT METHODS OF MEDITATION

It is important to sample the various methods of meditation before deciding on the one which suits you.

Give each one a fair trial, perhaps practising it ten minutes a day for a week, before moving onto the next. I have known plenty of students who came to my classes expecting to respond to quiet contemplation, for example, but who found themselves hooked by the inner visions that arose during creative visualization exercises.

GOOD MEDITATION PRACTICE

There are several points to bear in mind before you start meditating on a regular basis.

• Consider keeping a journal of your experiences and insights as the significance of certain details may only become apparent after subsequent sessions.

• It is not a good idea to eat a heavy meal if you are planning to meditate within the next hour as the physiological functions slow down the digestion.

• Because of the descriptive detail in many of the exercises it is a good idea to record the script so that you do not have to break your concentration to refer back to the instructions. However, with regular practice you should eventually be able to go through the sequence of the simpler exercises from memory.

• If you feel anxious or uncomfortable for any reason during meditation remember that you are not going anywhere, so there is no need for fear. Meditation is not a form of mediumship. You are not dabbling in the occult, communicating with spirits or anything similar. You are going inwards in search of self-awareness and greater understanding for your own highest good. However, if you do feel uneasy for any reason during a meditation simply count down slowly from ten to one and return to waking consciousness. If you do this you will invariably find that the anxiety goes before you open your eyes and so you can continue the exercise.

• Meditation is perfectly safe unless you have a history of psychological problems or are taking drugs or strong medication.

• There is a lot of talk about the 'Inner Child' nowadays, but you have to remember that this child is all ego and it does not want to grow up! It may play tricks from time to time in an attempt to disrupt your concentration. Do not be surprised if you find yourself worrying whether a spider might be crawling around while you have your eyes closed, or if you begin to have doubts about the time you are spending in meditation when you could be doing something else. When these thoughts occur simply bring your attention gently back to the subject of the exercise.

• Unexpected noises can be a distraction, but only if you let them. The banging of a door, a car horn and so on are gone in a moment, but if you worry about how you might react if it happens again, or despair of getting perfect peace and quiet, you empower them with life beyond that moment. It is comparatively easy to meditate in perfect silence, the real test is to remain relaxed and focused in the real world.

• Finally, ensure your privacy and peace as much as possible. Take the phone off the hook or put the answering machine on, and put a sign on the door telling flatmates or family that you are not to be disturbed.

'If you spent one-tenth of the time you devoted to distractions, like chasing women or making money, to spiritual practice, you would be enlightened in a few years!' (Ramakrishna)

Right: Recording your impressions of meditation in a journal is a good way to focus your thoughts, analyse your insights and to establish the routine of daily practice.

creating sacred spaces

'Ritual is meditation expressed in action.'

(Dion Fortune)

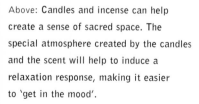

Above: Candles and incense can help create a sense of sacred space. The special atmosphere created by the candles and the scent will help to induce a relaxation response, making it easier to 'get in the mood'.

Meditation can be practised wherever and whenever you feel the need to create a quiet moment, although obviously there are times when you need to be alert and attentive such as when you are driving a car or working with machinery. Otherwise, it can be beneficial to establish brief mindfulness meditations during a lull at work or a break from routine tasks and long periods of study. You can even meditate while walking (see page 52). However, most of your practice will presumably be done at home, and although it is not necessary to dedicate a special room or corner of your living space for meditation there are many benefits to be derived from having a special place where you can practise.

CHOOSING YOUR SPACE

The first benefit of having a regular place to meditate is that it helps to establish the routine and break the initial resistance which everybody has to sitting still and staying silent for more than a few minutes. Creating a simple altar, if you desire one, and decorating the area in a suitably calming or neutral colour with pictures and objects that are designed to put you 'in the mood' will make a room feel like your private sanctuary, and will put passive pursuits like watching TV into a new perspective.

The second reason for having a dedicated space is that you will find that the room will soon acquire an ambience that is conducive to meditation and relaxation as it will have been 'charged' by your positive mental energy. Each time you enter the room you will intuitively tune in to these subtle vibrations and find that you settle into meditation more easily as a result of this inviting, therapeutic atmosphere.

Below: A small altar can be a positive focus for meditation.

MAKING YOUR SANCTUARY

Everyone has their own idea of what an ideal sanctuary might look like for them, but here are a few helpful hints.
• Keep the room simple. Bear in mind that the primary aims of meditation are heightened concentration and total absorption in a single idea or object, both of which you will find difficult to achieve in a room that is too cluttered with New Age bric-a-brac.
• An altar can be a useful focus for meditation, and can be decorated with candles, a statuette, a picture or symbols of the elements.
• Try limiting yourself to a single central object such as a small picture or a statue of Buddha or another deity that you can focus upon without distraction and who will induce a sense of the sacred and spiritual.
• Have something from nature within reach, such as a bowl of water, a small vase of flowers or a pot plant that could act as a focal object in a specific exercise or as an offering to the 'Universal Force'.
• Symbols of the four elements are also useful tools for contemplation. Represent Earth with a crystal, salt or a plant; Air with incense; Fire with a candle; and Water with a full ceramic bowl of it. If you do not have a crystal the bowl will double as Earth as it does in many traditions.
• To add symbols of the primary principles (male and female, negative and positive, active and passive) two candlesticks will suffice, or you can include images of the sun and moon.
• If you are using candles, always make sure that they are secure and that the holder is placed in a large bowl of water so that there is no risk of fire.
• The room needs to be comfortably warm and well aired, particularly if you are using candles or incense which use up oxygen and can leave you feeling tired.
• Wind chimes and soothing music or natural sounds can help create the right atmosphere, but if you are using music or pre-recorded visualizations, be sure to vary them so that you are not tied to one particular theme or exercise for too long.

Of course, you do not need to have a dedicated space for meditation and in time, with regular practice, you will create a sanctuary in your mind so that it will have a reality on the inner levels. As for being able to generate sacred space, you already do this with the influence of the aura that you radiate and that is why it is important that you create an aura of peace in meditation so that you can take it with you out into the world.

getting off the ground

This section describes the principles of posture and breath control before presenting a set of simple meditations to help establish the habit and the foundations of good practice. These preliminary exercises will help you to develop greater powers of visualization, concentration and deep relaxation as well as an acute awareness of the mind and physical body in action. The distinction between active and passive meditation is also outlined together with a look at how to bring meditation into daily life through a form of heightened awareness known as 'mindfulness'. The section ends with bodyscanning and grounding exercises to reduce stress and centre you in preparation for more advanced techniques.

posture

Above: THE EGYPTIAN POSITION
This traditional posture is ideal for the beginner as it is simple and easy to sustain over a long period.

Above right: FULL LOTUS POSITION
For the full lotus position, place your right foot on your left thigh and your left foot on your right thigh. Rest your palms on your knees. This ensures circulation of energy around the body.

When you first start meditating, it is important to try to establish good habits early on, specifically those concerning correct posture and breath control. However, do not become too preoccupied with details. Aim to ease yourself into meditation so that relaxation and serenity soon come as readily as sleep.

Many of the exercises in this book are concerned with stimulating the free flow of energy around the body and of drawing the 'universal life force' that we can all have access to into the head and through the feet. For that reason those meditations should be performed when sitting down. However, general relaxations and visualizations can be performed lying flat on a bed or mat if you prefer.

LYING DOWN

If you choose to lie down, lie on an exercise mat or a carpet and make sure that you support your neck with a firm cushion. Let your arms hang loosely by your side and keep your legs straight. Do not cross your legs or put your hands on your body unless you want to use your hands to direct healing energy to a particular area.

SITTING DOWN

Choose a straight-backed chair to sit in so that you get support and do not cramp your diaphragm. Your feet should be flat on the floor and slightly apart in line with your shoulders. Place your hands on your knees, palms down, although you may prefer to have them facing upwards in a symbolic gesture of openness or to send out energy during absent healing. Some people like to adopt the Buddhist practice of cupping their hands in their laps in front of their navels with the tips of their thumbs touching, but such details are a matter of personal choice. As a general rule do whatever feels right and is comfortable for you.

Do not let your chin sink into your chest because it will restrict your breathing. Your chin should be just slightly inclined towards your chest, while you look straight ahead.

CLASSICAL POSTURES

The traditional cross-legged postures that are used in yoga and Buddhism require a degree of suppleness that does not come easily to Westerners. However, you can train yourself to adopt these positions which you may feel enhances the meditation experience.

The classical postures are described within the captions to the pictures on these two pages, but an alternative position is to rest on your heels with a cushion supporting the buttocks, as in the Japanese tradition described in alternative postures overleaf.

Far left: HALF LOTUS POSITION
For the less demanding half lotus position, the right foot rests on the left thigh while the left foot lies under the right thigh, or vice versa. Palms can be turned upwards in a receptive gesture or cupped around the knees.

Left: QUARTER LOTUS POSITION
This is particularly suitable when you wish to emphasize your openness, i.e. for guidance, self-healing and cleaning meditations.

alternative postures
and hand positions

Although the various postures described and illustrated on these pages are interchangeable, you should attempt all of them initially, persevering with each for a week until settling with one or two that you find particularly suitable. The purpose of the various postures is to discipline the body in the belief that the mind will follow. As you focus your attention on the physical demands of the increasingly difficult positions, the mind will cease its restless chatter, and you will become mindful of the body and centred more effectively than if you simply sit in a chair and relax.

Both posture and breath are useful for aiding concentration when your thoughts wander, as they will do in the early stages of meditation. This centring of mind and body will also influence your performance during your daily activities. You will become more confident and efficient because your mind and body are being integrated at the deepest level. Being poised in this way

Below: JAPANESE — **Support your back
by resting your bottom on a firm cushion.**

Below: HEELS TOGETHER — **The inverted
heel focuses energy in the sacral chakra.**

will also help to create a sense of space within yourself where the real work will take place.

Exercise: The ideal image

Choose one of the positions from described in this chapter and then sit or lie down as preferred, close your eyes, relax and visualize yourself sitting before a large mirror in which is reflected the image of a figure in the position you have chosen. He or she is surrounded by coloured candles and wisps of scented incense smoke. Now look into the world beyond the mirror where the faceless figure lives. It is a serene scene with lush-green valleys and snow-capped mountains in the far distance. Feel yourself being drawn out of your body to merge with this figure. Feel the poise, the serenity that comes from being centred, and the expanding awareness as your mental energy transcends the limitations of your physical body. When you feel ready, gradually return to waking consciousness.

Below: CROSS-LEGGED – The cupped hands encourage energy to build in the solar plexus.

Above: The position of the hands can enhance the feeling of relaxation and awareness.

Above: Cradling one hand in the other symbolizes the active hand becoming passive under the influence of the non-active hand.

Above: Closing the thumb and forefinger symbolizes the completion of the energy cycle and wholeness.

the breath of life

Without a doubt the most difficult aspect of meditation to master is the quietening of the mind. Even when we are physically relaxed our minds are still buzzing. Until we can control this restless activity and learn to focus our mental energy it will be diffused and we will have passed the time reserved for meditation, rather than having used it.

The simplest method of stilling the mind is to focus on a single object or action, for it is impossible to concentrate on two things at the same time. We focus naturally when something interests us, but usually the object of interest is not suitable for meditation. In theory, of course, everything is a suitable subject for meditation, but it is best to keep it simple. That is one reason why the first step is to learn basic breath control.

BASIC BREATH CONTROL

Aim for a regular rhythm which you can help to establish by counting at your own tempo.

- Close your eyes and become aware of your breathing.
- Place your hands in front of your navel and feel your diaphragm move out as you inhale (**1** opposite).
- Move your hands to your chest and feel your lungs expand (**2**).
- With outstretched arms exhale gradually and inhale deeply without forcing the air in or out (**3**).
- Now take as deep a breath as you can comfortably manage, hold it for a count of 4, then let it out like a sigh as slowly as you can until every last particle of bad air has been expelled from your lungs.
- Now begin to establish a regular rhythm using either a count of 4-2-4-2 or 8-4-8-4. That is, inhaling for a count of 4, holding that breath for a count of 2 before exhaling for a count of 4, then pausing for a count of 2 before taking the next breath.

If you find counting too mechanical you can exchange it for a mantra (see page 98) or a simple spoken phrase such as 'peace and calm'. After a few months it should be easy to maintain the rhythm without counting.

When you eventually meditate without counting or using a mantra you will find that thoughts arise in the silence. It is then that you will have to cultivate the discipline of detachment by allowing thoughts to arise, observing them without becoming distracted and then returning to the object that you have chosen to focus upon.

ADVANCED BREATHING TECHNIQUE

Alternate nostril breathing is central to yogic meditation and is proven to be effective in dealing with stress. The techniques given here are adapted from classical yoga and are best performed in the lotus position or cross-legged:

- Keeping the three main fingers of your right hand closed, extend your thumb and little finger (**1a**). With the right nostril blocked by your thumb, breathing deeply inhale for five seconds and exhale for five through the left nostril.
- Bring your fourth or your little finger across to block your left nostril, then release your thumb (**2a**).
- Inhale for five seconds and exhale for five seconds through the right nostril (**3a**). Repeat the exercise 10 times on the right nostril and 10 times on the left. Next, try inhaling for five seconds, holding for three seconds and exhaling for five seconds. Repeat 10 times on each nostril.

Another variation is as follows:

- Close your eyes and put your thumb against your right nostril. Place your index and middle fingers over your 'third eye', (situated in the middle of your forehead) while your fourth and little finger rest against your left nostril.
- Breathe deeply, exhale then close your right nostril with your thumb. Now gently and deeply ingale through your left nostril for eight seconds. Hold that breath for four seconds and close your left nostril with the fourth finger. Keeping your left nostril closed, release the thumb and slowly exhale for eight seconds through the right nostril.
- Inhale again through the right nostril for eight seconds. Hold the breath for four seconds and close both nostrils briefly. Open your left nostril and exhale for eight seconds. Begin the cycle again by inhaling through your left nostril.

Try to establish a smooth and regular rhythm. Repeat five times, then rest your hand on your knee and sit in silence for a few minutes.

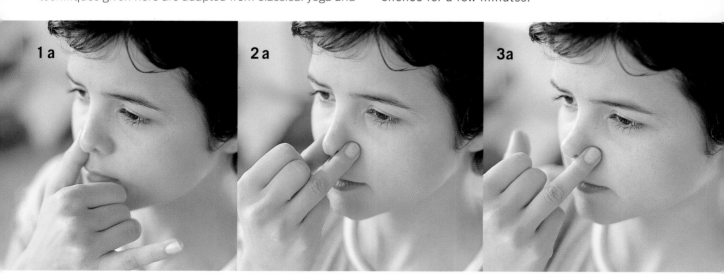

1a 2a 3a

active and passive meditation

Right: Take time out to scan your body for tension and give your mind a rest as it is in stillness that inspiration and insight will come.

'Yoga is the settling of the mind into silence. When the mind has settled, we are established in our essential nature, which is unbounded consciousness.' (Patanjali)

Practitioners of traditional yoga make a distinction between what they call active and passive meditation. Active is defined as the type that is practised while you go about your daily life approaching every experience as a meditation and observing your mind and body in action, while passive requires that you sit still, enter deep relaxation and concentrate.

We tend to think of meditation only in terms of the latter with its emphasis on solitude, stillness and silence, but active meditation is of equal importance in assimilating the benefits of meditation into everyday life.

OBSERVING THE BODY IN ACTION

We all have nervous habits of one kind or another, even if it only amounts to fidgeting while waiting for a bus, but such compulsions to keep active have a debilitating effect on our reserves of vital energy. Instead we should be conserving this energy, while remaining mentally alert. Relaxation is not just for those moments when we are doing nothing, but should be incorporated into our physical activities so that we can be productive with the minimum of effort.

Start to observe yourself at random points throughout the day and, if you find yourself fidgeting or sitting in an awkward posture, run through one of the simple head-to-toe relaxation exercises that you will find later in this book (see pages 44–45) and get your energy flowing freely again.

You will also find that you have more energy if you minimize the small talk that is believed to fritter away the life force. As has often been said, many of us talk a lot but say very little worth hearing. We tend to make small talk to fill the silence, but it is only in the silence that inspiration and insights can be heard.

OBSERVING THE ORDINARY MIND

Whether your daily routine tends to be repetitive and mundane or stimulating and stressful, you will learn much about yourself by becoming an observer of what is known as the ordinary, conscious mind, the 'I' with which we readily identify, or what orthodox psychology terms the ego. Note when it is concentrated on a task, or wandering, because when it is unfocused you are wasting vital mental energy.

Are you spending too long doing whatever task you have to do and is the end result a disappointment because you are unable to concentrate? Do you indulge in aimless wish-fulfilment, or in self-criticism over past mistakes? Do you fantasize about the future then fail to take the necessary steps to nurture these seeds to fruition?

Such problems stem from a lack of focus in life and a lack of control over the thought processes. We may all possess brains with the capacity of a supercomputer, but in practice our thoughts tend to get stuck in a groove like a stylus in an old vinyl record, playing the same old song until even the most negative thoughts have a familiar and comfortable ring about them. Becoming aware of the way in which the conscious mind undermines our efforts is the first step towards training the mind so that we can

free ourselves from such bad habits and tap into our subconscious and hidden potential.

When you become aware of negative thoughts do not let them run amok in your mind. Corner them and affirm that you disown such debilitating ideas.

While we know the value of physical relaxation we tend to keep the mind switched on in the same way that some people keep the radio running from breakfast to bedtime in the hope that something interesting will eventually come on. But just as tension in the body can leave us tired and strained, so the mind too, when burdened with anxieties and in need of rest can cease to function efficiently. So make time for mental as well as physical relaxation or you risk potential overload. It is said that 'those who have no time for meditation will have plenty of time for sickness and suffering.'

'Take rest; a field that has rested yields a

beautiful crop.' (Ovid)

mindfulness

'...in everyday life we rarely pay full attention to anything, whereas in meditation practice we commit ourselves exclusively to doing just that. When you pay full attention to anything (or to nothing), it becomes a spiritual practice.'

(Dan Millman, *Everyday Enlightenment*)

When the former world champion athlete Dan Millman was asked if his elite Stanford University gymnastics team in California in the USA practised meditation before a competition he replied that they did not; they actually meditated during the event. Millman had coached his team from bottom-of-the-league no-hopers to envied contenders for the national championship using a form of Zen Buddhist meditation known as mindfulness.

WHAT IS MINDFULNESS?

Mindfulness is one of the simplest meditation techniques and potentially the most revealing as it involves letting go

Opposite: **Every routine task, from preparing food to ironing clothes, can be used as the focus for meditation.**

Right: **If we can train ourselves to eat in a state of mindfulness, we will enjoy our food and derive more nourishment from it.**

of any desire to control your thoughts. Instead, you observe them with detachment as they arise spontaneously together with any emotions, physical sensations, sounds and images that compete for your attention. You attach no importance to them because if you allow yourself to be distracted they will assume a significance that they do not deserve. In effect, you accept no responsibility for your thoughts, but consider them to be insignificant because they have no intrinsic reality.

Millman observed, 'You don't have to control your thoughts, you just have to stop letting them control you.' He likens the mind to a barking dog and says that instead of trying to subdue it we should get on with whatever we are doing and let the dog bark, because that is what dogs do.

To find lasting peace of mind we first have to accept that we cannot control our thoughts, only our response to them, and in doing so we make peace with our minds. Eventually, you should come to an understanding of the nature of mind through such meditations and find freedom from its content, for the mind deceives by creating the illusion that we can return to the past or anticipate the future using memory and imagination. But, in fact, we exist only in the present. That is the nature of consciousness and the one reality that we can experience in mindfulness meditation.

Some people who have difficulty with more 'conventional' forms of meditation which demand that we master our mental processes find mindfulness easier because it acknowledges that we cannot control our thoughts. Instead we watch them flit across our mental screen like birds in flight while we remain focused on a fixed point on the horizon.

TIP

At random moments during the day stop whatever you are doing and consider if you are in a mindful state of awareness. Are you physically relaxed and paying attention to the task in hand, or are you tense and anxious to finish it and move on to something else? Take a deep breath, hold it for a few moments then exhale it slowly. Now continue with what you were doing, but be mindful and live for the moment.

USING MINDFULNESS

You can practise mindfulness in the traditional sitting posture if you prefer, but you should try to practise it when doing things that require your full attention such as eating. Eating is a particularly good example of something that should be performed in the mindfulness state because only in that state will we really enjoy our food and derive the most nourishment from it.

Ultimately, every act from routine chores to making love should be performed in this relaxed state of awareness.

As a modern master of meditation, Sogyal Rinpoche, has written, 'Everything can be used as an invitation to meditation.'

simple meditations

Above and right: **Keep your initial exercises simple and ease into the habit of regular practice.**

'If the mind is not contrived, it is spontaneously blissful, just as water, when not agitated, is by nature transparent and clear.'

(Traditional Tibetan saying)

In meditation, as in other mental and physical disciplines, it is important to begin with simple exercises to establish good practice. These basic meditations will help you to establish the habit of sitting still in silence and will train your mind to focus on the object of the exercise. If you attempt the more demanding disciplines, such as guided visualizations, before you are comfortable with the basic techniques, then you may find that your mind wanders. You may also find that the quality of relaxation and awareness is diminished or unsatisfactory and that consequently you will not be able to trust the guidance and insights that may come through.

Choose one of these exercises and practise it once or better still twice a day for six days, then rest for one day before moving onto the next exercise. After you become comfortable with them all and you can retain the images in your mind for at least five minutes, move on to experiment with other techniques, but use these freely whenever you need to test your powers of concentration, or you need a few minutes of quiet for yourself during the day.

If you wish, they can also become part of your regular routine as supplements to the main meditations as they will prepare the mind for deeper relaxation and explorations into the subconscious.

Exercise: Dot meditation

Get into your chosen position (see pages 30–33). Close your eyes, breathe naturally (see pages 34–35) and when you feel suitably relaxed begin to visualize a tiny white dot directly in front of you against the darkness. If this is difficult at the beginning you can imagine a white chalkmark on a blackboard instead, but if you have to resort to this do not be distracted by other details that may intrude such as the stick of chalk itself, a hand drawing the chalkmark or even the entire schoolroom. The mind does not readily settle for simplicity, so do not encourage it to be creative at this point in your practice.

When you have the dot fixed in your mind for several minutes without distraction, then visualize it growing larger and larger until you can step into it. At this point open your eyes and sit still for a few moments before returning to what you were doing previously.

Try substituting the dot with a number the next time you attempt this exercise and when you have mastered that try to visualize a coloured circle or light. It is not as easy as you think and you may find these exercises boring, but it is vital that you develop these basic skills before you move on.

Exercise: Candle meditation

Sit in your chosen position and breathe naturally. Focus on a lighted candle and soften your gaze so that you are looking slightly beyond the flame. When you feel that you have retained it in your mind's eye, close your eyes and keep the flame as steady as you can. At first the afterglow will fade and you will be left with nothing, so you will need to open your eyes again and repeat the process.

Eventually you will have a mental image of the candle that is distinct from the afterglow and you should be able to retain this for some minutes. When you achieve this level of concentration let go and lose yourself in the flame. Become one with the flame so that there is no space between it and you. Enjoy the sense of spaciousness and expansion.

When you feel ready, slowly come back to waking consciousness and open your eyes.

focusing on inanimate objects

Centre and right: The objects of a 'still life' meditation should be kept as simple as possible.

Inanimate objects are commonly used as a focus for meditation in both the Eastern and Western traditions. You will need to incorporate a 'still-life' meditation in your own routine from time to time as it helps to develop the ability to meditate with your eyes open which, in time, will evolve into the discipline of heightened awareness known as mindfulness (see pages 38–39).

USING SIMPLE OBJECTS

Initially, choose a simple object with as few features as possible, such as an apple, a paperweight or a vase. If you decide to focus on a plant choose a simple form with one colour. You can increase the complexity of the objects in due course as your ability develops, but do not choose something that has any significance for you as

Do not try to memorize its features, but just observe it as if it is a bud that is going to blossom, or a musical box that will play an enchanting melody.

Allow the background to fade into soft focus as you zoom in on the object with the clinical detachment of a camera lens. Become acutely aware of its texture, colour and form. It is important to take your time as you do this. Do not let yourself become impatient to move on to the next part of the exercise. The object is not going anywhere.

Visualize yourself touching it, tasting it and smelling it; again, take your time. This is not a chore that needs to be done, it is the doing that is the whole purpose of the exercise.

This is a good point at which to end the meditation when you are a beginner (go to the countdown at the end), but when you feel ready to go further than this you can add the following stages.

Imagine that you have been shrunk to the size of an ant and can explore the object. Look back from that perspective and see yourself sitting in the chair. If this is difficult at first, persevere, as this ability to develop a sense of detachment and focus your awareness elsewhere is important.

Imagine the processes that were involved in manufacturing or growing this object and then the stages involved in bringing it to you. Visualize its part in the hierarchy of nature, the forces that brought it into being and the purpose of its existence. Even a paperweight or a pebble have a purpose and an indispensable place in existence, for everything in existence is interconnected. As you become aware of this the boundary between the objective and subjective will become blurred and you will become part of what you perceive. As your awareness increases, the object will become suffused with meaning.

Perceiving objects with the eyes of your spiritual side, your 'Higher Self', reveals an infinite chain of events and correspondences and the knowledge that everything is an indispensable particle in the pattern of existence.

When you are ready, return to waking consciousness by counting down from ten to one and stamping your feet to reaffirm your return to the physical world.

you do not want to be distracted by memories or images associated with the object.

Place the object just beyond arm's length so that it is situated between eye level and that of the navel when you are seated, so that you do not put any strain on your neck when looking down it for any length of time. Ensure that you place it on a plain surface that is clear of all other items, otherwise you might be distracted and unable to concentrate on the chosen object.

Exercise: Focusing on an object

Get into your chosen position. Close your eyes, take a deep breath, hold it for a few moments, then exhale slowly. When you feel sufficiently relaxed, open your eyes and soften your gaze as you focus on the object.

relaxing your body

The following exercise is a highly effective method of gaining relief from stress. It can be practised while lying in bed before falling asleep or at any time when you want to achieve deep relaxation. It is effective because it acknowledges that we all generate a degree of tension, and in accepting it, rather than struggling against it, we can attune ourselves more effectively to the needs of the body and so relax more deeply.

Exercise: Working through the body

Get into your chosen position. Begin by closing your eyes and focusing on your breathing. Feel the weight and warmth of your body. As you relax deeper into yourself, you will feel heavier as the warmth begins to envelop you.

When you feel comfortable take a deep breath and sigh, releasing all the air from your lungs. Now, starting with your scalp, work your way methodically down your body until your reach your toes, tensing each and every muscle. As you tense the muscle, hold it for a few moments and as you do so sense your focus shifting to that area of your body. Then relax. Let go and feel the healing heat of the 'Universal Force' being absorbed into every cell at that point.

Next wrinkle your forehead in an exaggerated manner, hold it and as you do so consider how unattractive worried and very serious people look in contrast to those who take life more lightly. Now let the tension go and relax. Next clench your teeth, hold that tension, then relax.

Tense your facial muscles by 'pulling a face', hold it, then relax. Few of us realize how tense we are until we exaggerate it in this way. You may have thought you were relaxed before you began this exercise, but scanning the body in this methodical manner should make you more aware of how tense you often are without realizing it.

Now think of something that will make you smile. Better still, think of something that will make you laugh. Meditation is not something to be endured as a solemn ritual. You often see Buddhist monks laughing or smiling as if they are enjoying a private joke. If you want to share their joy all you have to do is take yourself lightly as they do and live for the moment.

Now focus on your neck and shoulders. Hunch the shoulders as high as you can, hold them there, then relax. Tense, hold and then relax your upper arms, then do the same with your lower arms, before clenching your fists – hold and then relax.

Now tighten your chest, hold and then relax. Then focus on the solar plexus area in the centre of your stomach. Hold your stomach in, and as you do so sense the heat in the solar plexus intensifying and beginning to spread through the upper and lower back. Now let it out and relax.

As the heat massages the muscles in your back, tense your lower back, hold it and sense the healing warmth being absorbed into the tissues. Sense your body becoming heavier as the warmth radiates outwards saturating your body in a golden glow.

Tense the buttocks, hold and then relax. Then do the same with the thighs and the calf muscles in the lower legs. Move down to your feet. Draw them in the direction of your upper body as if straining to see them, then release all the tension. Curl your toes, hold them and then relax.

Finally, gradually bring the focus of your attention back up to your head, and as you do so draw the warmth up through your body until it fills every particle with radiant energy and vitality. You are now fully relaxed, but still acutely aware of your surroundings. If you wish, allow yourself to drift off to sleep or return gradually to waking consciousness by counting down from ten to one.

1 Scanning your body for tension can make you aware how subtle stress can affect us all.

2 Scan your body methodically in your mind, tightening and then relaxing each muscle as you do so.

3 Acknowledge and accept a certain degree of tension, do not fight it.

warm up

Although a physical warm-up routine may appear superfluous to your meditation practice, it is useful in freeing energy blockages which tend to occur in the head, neck and back. We usually remain unaware of these blockages until we focus on this area. Warming up loosens the muscles and gives a sensation of expansion and openness. Relaxation and breath control will be more difficult to achieve if the body is cramped and allowed to slump or slouch. The neck, head and shoulders tend to lock-up with tension and stress. A few simple warm-up exercises will help to loosen these muscles and will open the upper body in readiness for deep relaxation.

3

4

1–4 Move your head forwards and backwards before finishing with a few side movements tilting your right ear to your right shoulder, then doing the same with the left.

5

5 Finally raise both shoulders as high as you can, tense the muscles, hold for a few moments and relax. Then roll the shoulders a few times, first forwards and then backwards.

1a Wrinkling your forehead will help dissipate tension and stress.

2a Clenching your teeth and pulling a face heightens awareness of stress and can lighten you up.

how to achieve deep relaxation

The following exercise can be used as an extension to the Relaxing Your Body Meditation, or it can be done on its own whenever you feel the need to get away from it all, mentally, physically and emotionally. It should be performed lying down.

Exercise: The Lagoon

Lie down comfortably. Close your eyes and begin by focusing on your breathing.

Inhale as deeply as you can, then let the air out in a long, slow breath. Pause before taking the next breath and sense the stillness and silence of that moment. Take another deep breath, pause again and sink into that silence. Now take regular breaths pausing for a few moments as you inhale and exhale. Each time you do this try to immerse yourself in those moments when

there is no movement in the body and no sound, not even of your own breathing.

Establish a regular rhythm then, when you are suitably relaxed, imagine that you are lying on a raft of soft reeds in a quiet lagoon. See the blue, almost cloudless, sky above, sense the gentle undulations of the water and listen to the sound of jungle birds calling in the distance. In the silence between the calls of the birds you catch the rustle of leaves on the far bank as a cooling breeze sweeps in from the sea. You hear a droplet of moisture fall from a leaf and splash in the sparkling blue water, then you hear another. With the sound of each droplet you are becoming more and more relaxed. The sound is so small that you have to strain to hear it and as you do you sink deeper and deeper into a profound state of relaxation.

You can feel the sun touching your body with its healing rays and warming the water. Feel the soothing heat gradually building to form what feels like a cushion of air supporting your back. The warmth makes you feel as if you are floating on a cloud as you sink deeper into relaxation, deeper than you have ever experienced before.

Only the occasional passing cloud gives you a sense that anything is moving in this secluded tropical paradise. A bird circles overhead as you gaze lazily into the azure blue sky. To the left and right you catch a glimpse of overhanging palm trees.

The scent of tropical plants is intoxicating, the blur of colours that you catch as you look from bank to bank are indeed the vivid colours of paradise. You are losing all sense of time for this is a place out of the normal world where your cares have no meaning. You simply exist to experience and enjoy the sights, sounds, smells and tastes of this secluded world. Listen to the sound of the water returning to its source, the sea, and allow yourself to flow with it as if you were floating on a leaf.

You are relaxed and exhilarated at the same time. The sun sparkles on the water like diamonds and you close your eyes to avoid the glare.

The current carries you into the shade of a large cave where fruit and jugs of fresh water have been left for your nourishment. Eat and drink your fill, and when you are satisfied make your way towards the light that is breaking through at an opening at the back of the cave. As you emerge into the light become aware of your surroundings, feel the weight of your body on the bed or the floor and slowly open your eyes.

how to centre yourself

This is a type of 'warming-up' exercise for deeper meditations and involves further visualization techniques. It can be used at a time of extreme emotional stress when you feel the need to bring yourself back down to earth, to 'centre' or ground yourself. Perform this exercise while sitting in a chair with your back straight and your feet flat on the floor.

Exercise: Grounding

Begin by focusing on your breathing. Breathe at your own pace in a rhythm of four-two-four-two; that is inhaling for a count of four, pausing at the top of the breath for a count of two, exhaling for a count of four and pausing once again between breaths for a count of two.

As you exhale, visualize the tension that has been trapped at various points in your body being released inside your body in the form of smoke. Visualize it as a form of energy pollution which you have involuntarily absorbed as you might do with exhaust fumes. With the tension of everyday living you have tightened up and trapped it in these pockets within your body. But now you are becoming aware that it is suffocating the 'Universal Force'.

You have no need of tension. It serves no useful function. See it seeping from your toes, your lower legs, your upper legs, the hips, the lower back and solar plexus (middle of stomach).

See it gathering in your stomach, rising up through your chest, neck, jaw and out through your nostrils with every exhalation. Visualize and sense it draining from your fingertips up into your lower arms, through your upper arms, into your neck, through your throat and out

'To know yourself is to forget yourself; To forget yourself is to be awakened by all things.'

(Dogen, Genjo Koen)

into the atmosphere. Finally, feel it seeping down from your forehead, where a band of tension created by worry and negative thoughts has held you in a vice-like grip, to your mouth. Free yourself from this tension by visualizing it dispersing like smoke with each out breath that you make.

Now that your head and body are clear once again you need to revitalize yourself with an infusion of the 'Universal Force'. Begin by visualizing a point just above your head and see a sphere of incandescent light appear like the sun in the noon sky. As you focus on this light with your inner eye it intensifies in brilliance. It descends upon you and you begin to inhale the light as you would fresh air or an intoxicating incense.

Absorb the energy as you breathe, and also through the crown of your head. Feel it relaxing your forehead, face and jaw. Feel the warmth saturating every cell of your being like an invigorating shower which cascades down your neck, through your arms to your hands and fingertips. It courses down through your chest, your stomach, solar plexus, hips, lower back and legs and rushes down to your toes. The light is cleansing and energizing. You feel refreshed, invigorated and renewed. Now there is nothing but the light circulating throughout your system.

This is the moment to send down roots of etheric energy into the earth to ground yourself so that you are not unbalanced by an excess of power. Do this by visualizing the energy seeping from the soles of your feet into the ground and forming roots. Sense yourself being anchored by them.

Now visualize a second sphere of almost translucent light like the full moon in the clear night sky emerging from the earth. Begin to draw this light up through the

TIP

Some people find themselves rocking back and forth during meditation, or they can become uncomfortably warm. This is because they have not grounded themselves properly and are unable to channel the excess energy which they have been bottling up and are now releasing. Using this grounding exercise on a daily basis will help you avoid this by channelling this etheric electricity safely into the earth rather like a lightning conductor.

soles of your feet and into your body. Sense the different quality of this energy rising up through your legs, hips, back, solar plexus and stomach. Sense it being soaked up by the cells in your fingertips, your hands, arms, chest, neck and head.

Feel the two streams of celestial and terrestrial energy blending in your physical body and permeating the other levels of your being. You are now fully energized and grounded.

Bathe in the light for as long as you wish, before slowly returning to waking consciousness by counting down slowly from ten to one. As you count down, focus once again on your breathing and become aware of your body, the chair you are sitting on and your surroundings. When you feel ready, open your eyes.

meditation in motion

'To calm your mind, go for a walk at dawn in the park, or watch the dew on a rose in the garden. Lie on the ground and gaze up into the sky, and let your mind expand into its spaciousness. Let the sky outside awake a sky inside your mind.' (Sogyal Rinpoche)

In the West we tend to equate meditation with sitting in silence, but there is a long tradition of walking meditations among spiritual seekers of all persuasions, from the religious pilgrim who travels vast distances to visit a shrine to the Burmese Buddhist monk who can take all day to cross a courtyard. Walking meditations as a formal discipline are thought to have developed after Buddha urged his followers to leave their homes in search of Enlightenment, and they continue to offer a counterbalance to the introspective practice of sitting in silence.

Many 'primitive' cultures mark the rite of passage from childhood to adulthood with a quest in which the youth must travel far from his community in order to discover himself. The Aborigines retain the ritual of the walkabout, the Native Americans send their sons on a spirit quest, while the West preserves the myth and romance of the quest for a magical relic, such as the Holy Grail, which is a symbol of the 'Higher Self'. And of course we all practise walking as a meditation whenever we decide to take a stroll to think things through.

Opposite, left: Be mindful of every movement as you walk rather than losing yourself in your own thoughts.

Opposite, right: During a walking meditation try and become acutely aware of your surroundings.

Exercise: A walking meditation

While it is not necessary for us to walk in as formal or deliberate a manner as the Burmese monk who is mindful of every movement of his feet, nor imitate the student of Zen who walks in a circle synchronizing each step, we need to be as acutely aware of our body when walking as we are of our environment. So be mindful of your posture and the way you carry yourself. You should be 'centred' (see page 50), poised and economical with your movements. You are not walking for exercise so do not put any effort into it. Establish a steady rhythm and allow the momentum to lull you into a relaxed state of awareness.

Avoid any distractions by focusing on a point directly ahead of you in the middle distance. Obviously, this is more practical if you are on a long straight track in the countryside or on the beach, but if you are having to negotiate a labyrinth of urban streets you simply change the object of your attention every time you turn into a new street.

Tune into a specific sound and replay it in your mind. It can be the roar of a car engine, the barking of a dog or the sound of the wind rustling the leaves in the trees. It might even be a snatch of conversation that you pick out in passing or the sound of your own footsteps. Regardless of whether it has a mechanical or natural origin it will have a dominant tone. Can you tune into it? And, when you have done so, can you retain its resonance in your mind?

Focus on a stationary object and try to retain its image for as long as you can after it has passed out of your field of vision. This will help develop your powers of visualization and you should find these images

coming vividly to mind during your nightly review (see page 74).

Make yourself acutely sensitive of all sensory input – the wind on your face, the crunch of gravel under your shoes, the quality of light, the collage of colours, any lingering smells, the taste of salt in the air if you are walking by the sea and the shifting balance in your body as you move.

Remember that the object of this exercise is to be mindful of your body and your surrounding environment. Do not let your mind wander and, if you find yourself becoming lost in thought, focus yourself gently back to a state of detached observation.

'Life was never meant to be a struggle, just a gentle progression from one point to another, much like walking through a valley on a sunny day.' (Stuart Wilde, *Affirmations*)

holistic
healing

This section explores how you can stimulate the subtle energy centres known in the Hindu tradition as the 'chakras' for the purposes of self-, absent and planetary healing. It also describes how you can channel this vital universal force to protect yourself from negative influences and revitalize yourself whenever you are stressed or depleted of energy. It concludes with a description of how the four elements correspond to aspects of the human psyche and outlines how you can work with these natural forces to increase your self-awareness and psychic sensitivity, or intuition.

self-healing and healing others

'All we need to receive direct help is to ask...And yet, asking is what we find hardest.'

(Sogyal Rinpoche)

It is now generally accepted that the cause of many physical disorders is a deeply rooted dis-ease in the mind or psyche, and not simply a random biological breakdown in the body. If this is so, then it should be possible to restore balance to the whole of our being by removing the blockage or blockages which we have created in order to draw attention to our unhappiness.

The first step towards self-healing is to acknowledge that we may have unconsciously manifested these symptoms because we fear the strength of our own emotions. If, for example, we lose a loved one and deny ourselves the cleansing process that is grief, then we risk suppressing those emotions and can restrict the free flow of the life force, creating a chemical imbalance that may eventually show itself as physical pain.

NEGATIVE EMOTIONS

If you doubt how destructive our thoughts and emotions can be, just recall how you felt the last time you were upset, angry or stressed. Do you remember how the negative thoughts or emotions made you feel physically uncomfortable as your muscles tensed and your blood pressure rose, draining you of vital energy and leaving you feeling despondent and dispirited?

When we feel content our mental energy is 'centred' (as it is in the chakras, our spiritual centres) and when we are excited or exercising our creative imagination it expands. But when we indulge in negative thoughts or are feeling stressed we restrict the flow of mental energy which leaves us literally depressed and may even manifest as physical pain or a headache.

HOW MEDITATION HEALS

Meditation helps to heal us because it can puts us back in touch with our emotions, thoughts and physical sensations. It also puts our impatience and intolerance into perspective and creates a sense of detachment which helps us keep a check on our emotions.

The chakra balancing (see pages 60–61) and Body of Light exercises (see pages 62–63) in this section are ideal for self-healing, but if you wish to give healing to another person in their presence, or in the form of absent healing, the following meditation will be suitable. However, healing of any kind should ideally be developed under the guidance of experienced teachers or masters.

Spiritual healing might not appear to be a meditation, but it is a perfect example of meditation in action. To attempt to heal other people, or at least to alleviate their suffering, is to practise a meditation on compassion, arguably the most direct path to Enlightenment.

HELPING TO HEAL ANOTHER

If you are giving someone a treatment ask them to remove their glasses if they are wearing any, but to remain fully clothed. Get them to sit in an open-backed chair or on a stool so that you can treat their back. If they prefer lying down, ask them to turn over when you need to do their back. If this is not possible you will have to visualize the healing force penetrating through the front of the body to permeate each and every cell until it is absorbed into the muscles of the neck, spine and back.

If you want to send absent healing to someone, simply visualize them sitting with their back to you and affirm

TIP
One important word of advice. Before you close down after a healing session always remember to recharge your own batteries by balancing your chakras or working through a revitalizing exercise such as The Body of Light (see page 62). When you are healing, you need to be an open and clear channel for the universal energy and not the source, so you need to be able to trust this energy to do its work and visualize it doing so (especially if, as sometimes happens, you do not feel any sensation yourself).

that they will receive this healing energy wherever they are at that moment.

It is not necessary to touch the person you wish to treat. You can just work on the spiritual aura that surrounds their physical body, but even then make initial contact by placing your hands on their shoulders until you feel you are in tune with them. They do not need to enter a meditative state, although of course they can if they wish to.

Exercise: Simple healing

Before beginning this exercise make sure you are grounded by working through the exercise described on page 50.

When you feel 'centred' and suitably relaxed, place your hands on the shoulders of the person you wish to heal and silently affirm your wish to be an open and clear channel for the universal healing energy. Acknowledge that you are not the source of this force and keep this in your mind as you direct the energy (which you might feel as heat or a tingling sensation in your hands) to the various parts of the body.

Meditate on compassion and sense the softening of the heart and solar plexus chakras (see pages 60–61) as you draw the healing light down through the crown of your head, and also up through your feet, and then out through the palms of your hands.

When you feel that the energy is flowing and that your auras have merged, start at the crown of the head and work your way down the person's body to the toes, giving equal emphasis to every area and smoothing the aura as you go. Become acutely aware of any areas that might feel cold or where you may sense resistance. The person you are treating may have indicated what their symptoms are, but it will not necessarily be where the source of the problem lies. The meditative state you are in will sensitize you to the still, small voice of your inner guide who may move your hands to where the healing needs to be concentrated.

It is important to see the healing process taking place and to picture the person you are treating in perfect health while you are giving them a treatment. But, whatever insights you gain, do not be tempted to make a diagnosis of their problems if you are not a fully qualified medical practitioner. Also do not make any claims to healing powers or make promises of any kind whatsoever. If you are successful they will feel better and you will benefit by having opened yourself to the 'Universal Force'.

End the session with a blessing or affirmation and let the person sit for a few moments to 'ground' them, in case they feel slightly unbalanced by the surge of energy that they have received.

If you are healing in person, or are in contact with someone who is elderly or ill, it is always a good idea to enter a meditative state even while you are talking to them. Ground yourself and always channel the energy so that you both can benefit. If you do not feel able to give healing for any reason, then at least protect yourself by visualizing a metal plate in front of your solar plexus or a ball of light encasing you from head to toe.

planetary healing

Many people that have come to my meditation classes tell me that they are badly affected by the terrible things that they see on the nightly TV news. They ask what they can do to unburden themselves of these sad feelings, and if there is something that they can do to help those who are suffering.

Exercise: Sending absent healing

If you are unable to give any practical help then sending absent healing will relieve you of any distress, and at the same time channel healing energy to where it is needed. All you have to do is close your eyes, relax and recall the haunting images that you saw. Do not try to control your feelings, but use them. If you try to suppress your emotions it could eventually create a blockage in your own system which will affect your

'By the virtue amassed by all that I have done,

May the pain of every being be completely headed,

May I be doctor and medicine, and may I be nurse,

For all sick beings in the world 'til all are well.'

(Excerpt from a poem and prayer by the Buddhist poet Shantideva, 8th century)

health. But if you use your emotions in this way to 'soften' the solar plexus and heart chakras the healing energy will be released naturally. All you will have to do then is to direct it using your imagination.

First ground yourself using the exercise on (page 50) and then imagine a small ball of warm, white light rotating in the centre of your solar plexus, the seat of your emotions. See it growing and intensifying until it merges with your heart centre in the middle of your chest, the place of your 'Higher Self' and of unconditional love. Now see this swirling whirlpool of energy emerge from your torso and drift out of your body to be beamed across the world to wherever you wish to direct it. See it illuminating the region you have chosen and being absorbed by the person or people who need it. Take your time to see the effect.

Now continue to watch as energy flows in from healers and healing groups all over the world who meditate on a daily basis with this same aim in mind. Join your energy with theirs. Sense the intensifying power as you link in with this surge of the natural creative force. Some of these individuals and groups focus on particular places because they are in the news, but many generate healing energy and send it in the belief that it will reach whoever needs it. If you are sending healing to a particular person, a friend or family member, be aware that you are not working alone. Draw upon this reservoir of energy created by the network of healers from around the world by visualizing yourself as part of a invisible grid criss-crossing the planet.

Zoom out to take in a view of the Earth as seen from space and watch as universal life energy rises from pinpoints of light across the globe to encase the Earth

in a matrix of glistening strands. When you feel that you have contributed all that you can, mentally close down your energy centres and then ground yourself symbolically by stamping your feet.

Exercise: Spreading the light

If you are concerned about negative influences in your own neighbourhood and beyond and you want to contribute to the raising of planetary consciousness you can use a variation on this meditation.

When you meditate, visualize yourself generating white light from a warm spot in your solar plexus. Visualize that light blending with light that you draw up from the ground through your feet and light that you draw down from the air.

When you feel 'centred' and energized, visualize that light spreading out from you like a beacon throughout your immediate environment. Visualize its blinding intensity spreading through the streets of your town and beyond through the county, across the country and, if you can sustain the image, beyond national borders to envelop the world. See it being absorbed into the ground and being soaked up by a thirsty earth. While you are channelling this energy say a prayer or affirmation which expresses your unconditional love for the planet and your fellow human beings to make you an even more open and efficient channel for the divine healing energy. When you are ready gradually return to waking consciousness.

working with the chakras

The following exercise is designed to activate the seven major chakras, the subtle spiritual energy centres in the etheric body, in sequence by visualizing them as blossoming lotus flowers in their appropriate colours. The word 'chakra' is derived from a Sanskrit word meaning 'wheel', and the chakras are believed to spin in a clockwise or anti-clockwise direction. The seven chakras working upwards from the feet are the base, sacral, solar plexus, heart, throat, third eye and crown chakra. These energy centres are also believed to be linked to the endocrine system, so working on the chakras can also benefit the physical body.

Ideally, this exercise should be done each morning to stimulate the circulation of energy through the chakras and to create a general sense of wellbeing. It can be performed either sitting in a chair or in the lotus position (see pages 30–31). However, it is not as effective when performed lying down.

Exercise: Chakra balancing

Close your eyes and begin by focusing on your breathing (see pages 34–35).

When you feel sufficiently relaxed, visualize a closed white lotus flower on the ground between your feet. Take your time and fix it firmly in your mind's eye in as much detail as you can. See the rich green leaves and the waxy white petals and sense the life force inside you begin to stir. Now watch closely as the lotus slowly opens to reveal petals flecked with a hint of brown and black. These are the lowest vibrations in the colour spectrum corresponding to the energy of the earth and the base chakra at your feet. Begin to feel this energy around your feet 'grounding' you in the earth, steadying you for the ascent in consciousness.

Now visualize a second lotus emerging from the sacral chakra beneath your navel. This second lotus is a vivid red. Red is the lowest vibration in the colour spectrum. It is the colour of physical energy. Watch as the lotus opens and feel the energy stimulating your sacral chakra and radiating outwards around your body.

Now visualize a third flower opening in your solar plexus chakra, the seat of your emotions. The petals of this lotus are orange. Orange balances the red of physical energy with the yellow of the mental level. As

the flower unfolds sense the energy in this chakra dissolving the tension and unravelling any knots that may have been in your stomach, trapping emotions which need to be released.

From the heart centre in the middle of your chest a fourth flower emerges, a white lotus with a yellow centre and petals that are tinted with streaks of green. Yellow is symbolic of the vital and healing force of the sun and of the intellect, while green is the colour of harmony and of nature. Green is also symbolic of the boundary between the physical and spiritual realms. As the petals open, sense the refreshing energy awakening the heart chakra, energy that flows instinctively in response to natural beauty and brings compassion for all living things.

The next lotus to materialize is in the throat centre. It has a violet and purple hue on the outer petals, but when it unfolds the inner leaves are veined with a vivid blue. Blue is the third primary colour and is the first of the spiritual colours. Blue presides over the passions and the mental processes. It is symbolic of the throat chakra through which we are able to express our thoughts and feelings. As the lotus opens, sense the energy stimulating this centre.

Then concentrate on the middle of your forehead and feel a tickly sensation as the sixth lotus in your third eye (brow) chakra opens. The petals are a vivid violet colour. This is our spiritual centre where we develop our imagination and latent clairvoyant abilities.

Finally, focus on a point just above your head traditionally designated as the crown chakra, and visualize a pure white lotus emerging into the light of the multi-coloured aura which now surrounds you. As you watch this symbol of the life force unfolding you sense the light in your lower chakras intensifying, rising in a stream of pure light and energy to revitalize every cell of your being.

This light then spills out of your crown chakra, bubbling over into your aura, bathing you in a cascade of pranic (universal) energy that refreshes, invigorates and cleanses you throughout your entire body. When the stream has run its course you are left in a deep state of relaxation free from the negativity of the physical world.

Gradually return to waking consciousness by counting slowly down from ten to one, refocusing on your breathing, and becoming aware once again of the weight of your body sitting in the lotus position or on a chair. If you are not going on to further spiritual work, go back through the chakras from the crown and visualize the lotus flowers closing. Then when you are ready slowly open your eyes.

Above: The seven chakras, the energy centres of the etheric body. Each is associated with a different spiritual and physical function.

the healing light

We have all been conditioned to believe that illness is inevitable and that it is only by maintaining a degree of physical fitness or taking prescribed drugs that we can fight infection or restore a breakdown in our biological functions. However, the basic principle of holistic health states that all physical symptoms are a manifestation of dis-ease in the emotional, mental or spiritual bodies and that we can eliminate illness, or at least limit its physical effects, by instilling our subconscious with positive life-affirming images.

WHY WE GET ILL

In some cases a person may show the symptoms of disease to substantiate their belief that they were for some reason destined to die from the same illness as other members of their family. Or they may create an imbalance in their body so that they do not have to face a difficult decision or situation. More commonly, illness can represent an inner conflict or a suppressed emotion which eats the healthy cells in the body like a parasite.

In every case meditation used on its own, or as a supplement to orthodox or complementary medicine, can help to relieve pain and reduce the anxiety which often aggravates the illness. It can also be used to reprogramme the subconscious mind so that negative thought patterns are effectively erased, making a recurrence of illness unlikely.

Exercise: Raising your energy

If you are ill, or just feeling run down and in need of revitalizing, the following exercise will help by stimulating every cell in your body and dissolving blockages which prevent the circulation of vital energy. It is also an ideal exercise to start the day, so try to fit it into your routine. Alternatively, if you need a boost at any time of the day, take five minutes out to raise your energy the natural way by following these simple steps, rather than drinking that extra cup of coffee or having a snack.

Get into your chosen position. Close your eyes and begin to focus on your breathing (see pages 34–35). Take a few deep breaths, then inhale deeply, hold it for a few moments, and then let the breath out as slowly and evenly as you can. Make a soft 'F' sound to push out the very last breath from the lungs so that you can start afresh.

Keeping a steady rhythm of breathing, begin to visualize a pool of soft white light at your feet. See it condensing like a luminous mist as you begin to draw it up around your ankles. Sense its gentle but penetrating warmth on the soles of your feet, then caressing your toes and your ankles as you begin to absorb the light into your body.

See and feel the warm, vibrant light soaking into your lower legs as if your skin were a sponge. The light is cleansing every cell and every blood vessel, stimulating the circulation of the subtle energies and the vital fluids as it rises from your knees up through your thighs to your hips and lower back.

Become aware of the light seeping into your lower and upper back, breaking up and dissolving any blockages there and allowing the free flow of vital energy to every cell in your system. Feel the light flowing into any remaining areas of tension and kneading the knots in your muscles until they are totally relaxed.

The light now flows through your arms to your hands and fingertips. See the light spreading out along the network of nerves and veins to your neck and into your head, relaxing your facial muscles and caressing your temples until you feel clear-headed and calm.

Your subtle, or etheric, body has become a body of light whose energy is radiating outwards to animate and purify every cell in your physical body.

When you feel ready, slowly open your eyes, but take a few moments to enjoy the peace before returning to your work or other tasks. Envisage this light surrounding you for the rest of the day.

the four elements

In the esoteric tradition the elements of Water and Earth are seen as symbols of the passive, feminine principle, while Fire and Air represent the active, masculine principle. For this reason meditating on the four elements can help to increase awareness of the essential constituents of our psyche.

Fire is traditionally seen as corresponding to the will, Air to the intellect, Water to the mutable emotions and Earth to the physical body. On a physical level these are expressed in finite form with Fire corresponding to bodily heat, Air corresponding to gases and breathing, Water corresponding to fluids and Earth corresponding to solid matter, such as the skeletal structure, the vital organs and muscles.

EARTH

When you meditate on the theme of Earth, a symbol of stability, it will help to strengthen the practical aspect of your nature. If your plans seldom see fruition, using a

visualization that is based on the construction of a cabin in a forest, or the establishment of a garden, for example, will help to focus your mind and encourage you to work through all the essential stages in your mind before embarking on a new venture.

Meditations with an Earth theme also reduce the risk of you becoming a 'bliss junkie', a state some people reach when they become addicted to the sense of detachment that meditation can bring. Some people have a tendency to use meditation to escape from responsibilities in the mistaken belief that being on a spiritual path means that they are more enlightened and thus relieved of obligations. However, the real value of meditation comes from bringing a greater awareness into daily life, not to escape from it.

AIR

The element of Air symbolizes both the intellect and prana, the animating spirit which manifests itself as the breath. Meditating on the breath can help to draw on

greater reserves of energy, revitalizing you if you have been ill and bringing serenity if you are under stress.

If your meditations contain images of strong, destructive winds then it could be that you are feeling insecure and at the mercy of your emotions. A visualization where you see yourself rising above the Earth in a balloon, or sailing through the skies as a bird, can help to detach you from your emotions, get a more realistic perspective on the situation, and clarify your thoughts so that you can make more rational decisions.

WATER

This is a traditional symbol of the emotions and in meditation it can also represent the unfathomable depths of the subconscious, fear of the unknown or of 'taking the plunge' into something new.

If you have a sense of being swept off course by the stormy waters of your own emotions, or if you feel 'out of your depth' in a situation, visualize the calm surface of the sea or a lake reflecting the moon which is itself a symbol of intuition. When you are ready, dip beneath the water and search for the answer you seek in the symbol of sunken treasure. When you return to the surface the significance of that symbol should be apparent.

FIRE

This element symbolizes both the purifying fire in which we can immerse ourselves during a meditation for the purposes of clearing persistent negative energies, and also the light of knowledge which can illuminate uncharted terrain in a pathworking visualization. The image of a flaming torch or lamp can be particularly useful if you want to explore memories and literally shed light on images from your past. These are best explored in the context of an attic or basement (both of which are symbols of the subconscious), but make sure that you are securely 'grounded' before exploring such potentially unsettling areas of the psyche.

becoming self-aware

'Accept with love the flaws of your friends and enemies, and you may learn to love and accept yourself.'

(Reshad Veild)

This exercise helps to develop your self-awareness by focusing the mind on the various elements that make up the body. It can also strengthen the relationship with nature and the outer world.

Exercise: Focusing on the four elements

Get into your chosen position. Close your eyes and focus on your breathing. Establish a regular rhythm, pausing at the top of each breath and again after exhaling. Think of your breathing as the element of Air within your physical being and consider that when you are tense you are restricting the flow of prana, the universal energy throughout the body, and that when you are in a hurry shallow breathing prevents this life force from reaching your vital organs. Decide that you will become more aware of your breathing from this moment forward.

Now consider the circulation of Air in the cycle of nature, how the plants, the insects, the birds and the animals are interdependent through their part in the process, and that even the creatures in the depths of the ocean are essential if the balance is to be maintained.

Next become aware of the skeleton which supports your body and the muscles that give you movement. Think of your bones, your muscles and your organs as the solid Earth element of your physical being and consider that these too need nourishment and nutrients to maintain the mechanical functions.

Next sense the blood circulating through your veins to the tiny network of capillaries which carry the oxygen to all your vital organs. Think of this as the Water element of your physical being. Now extend your

consciousness to the outside world and visualize the vital cycle of Water which replenishes the forests and the fields, the valleys and the mountains. See the trickling streams which bring essential minerals to fertilize the low lands and the dew hanging from the leaves of plants in the morning sunlight. In every droplet there is a rainbow as the light is refracted as if in a prism. See the full spectrum of colours and consider that even the smallest particle is an expression of the 'Universal Force'.

Now sense the heat in your skin which is generated in the tissues and consider that this regulation of body temperature is also vital in maintaining the life force and that it too functions without the need of your conscious mind. Think of this heat as the Fire element of your physical being.

Next become aware of the mineral element in your body in the bones, which appear solid but are continually growing. Think also of the basic minerals that you and everything in the universe are composed of, and how they also maintain the chemical balance in your body.

Now become conscious of the vegetable principle within you which governs growth, regeneration of the cells and the continuation of the species so that more souls can be born. Consider that these functions depend upon the four elements in the form of nourishment (Earth), light (Fire), Air and Water and resolve to be more mindful of them instead of taking them for granted. We can use even mundane things such as eating, drinking and breathing in a meditation and derive more nourishment for both body and soul by doing so.

Next become aware of the animal principle within – your vitality, curiosity, instinct, cunning, sociability and mobility. Consider where humanity would be without these attributes. Then become conscious of your uniquely human qualities – your imagination, inventiveness, memory, reflection and the ability to expand consciousness into the spiritual (higher) realms.

Finally, focus again on the four elements: the heat in your skin, the air in your lungs, the blood in your veins and the solidity of your bones which give you form.

When you are ready become aware of your surroundings and slowly open your eyes.

celestial bodies

If you meditate on the sun or moon, or if they appear spontaneously in a meditation, it can symbolize the blossoming of male or female qualities.

THE SYMBOL OF THE MOON

The moon is a universal symbol of the passive, feminine principle. Therefore meditating on the moon, or having it spontaneously appear during a meditation, can indicate the awakening of the feminine qualities of intuition, sensitivity, creativity and compassion in both men and women.

The full moon represents completion or wholeness and is widely associated with love, marriage and the family. It can therefore be quite useful to meditate on this image if you have to make a difficult decision regarding a relationship, although you must always balance what you

think is guidance from the subconscious with the conscious mind's common sense.

The ego is a great deceiver. We invariably believe what we want to believe and hear what we want to hear. Often what is 'right' for us is contrary to what we desire. Always test whatever comes through during meditation by asking yourself if it appeared spontaneously and if you were able to manipulate the images. If the imagery had a life of its own and you feel comfortable with it, then consider it as useful advice until you develop your intuition to the extent that you 'know' something has come from your 'Higher Self' and can act on it with confidence.

A female figurehead

Many psychologists would interpret the moon as being symbolic of a significant female figure, usually a sister, mother or partner whose influence is becoming stronger; or a person to whom you feel increasingly indifferent, for on an emotional level the moon is traditionally thought of as being 'cold'. If there is difficulty with a female figure in a relationship you can help to resolve it by visualizing yourself in the company of this person, preferably sitting by a lake in the moonlight and imagining a conversation with them. The setting will help to calm you and the image of the moon should stimulate the subconscious to bring all your thoughts on this subject to the surface.

You may have to 'write' the dialogue initially, but after a while the 'conversation' should become a natural, flowing exchange between your conscious and subconscious mind which may awaken feelings that you have not consciously expressed and might even offer solutions which you have not yet considered. Prepare to be surprised by yourself.

THE SYMBOL OF THE SUN

The sun is a universal symbol of the active, masculine principle, of the 'Universal Life Force', of healing, vitality and wisdom. Meditating on the sun, or having it appear spontaneously during a meditation, can indicate the awakening of the masculine qualities of vision, ambition and determination.

Orthodox psychology would interpret the appearance of the sun as a symbol of a father figure, a brother, a son or a male partner or close friend. For a man it can appear at a time when he needs to take on the role and responsibilities of his own father in order to be complete or when he needs to assert himself in an unequal relationship.

If the rising sun appears during meditation it can signify rebirth, the strengthening of the connection with your 'Higher Self', whereas the setting sun indicates the end of a specific phase in life and a need to rest before the next phase begins.

The sun for strength

If you are depleted of energy after a period of illness, feeling lethargic for any reason or have lost your enthusiasm for life you may find that meditating on the symbol of the sun will restore your strength. Simply imagine yourself in a beautiful garden or on a beach with the sun overhead and absorb its healing rays as if you were spiritually sunbathing. If you have an infection, whether it is a cold or something more serious, it can be beneficial to visualize the rays penetrating your skin and the sunlight being absorbed into your infected cells. See these as having a dark core and watch as the light burns them away until there is nothing left in your body but healthy cells.

'It is eternity now. I am in the midst of it. It is about me in the sunshine; I am in it, as the butterfly floats in the light-laden air.'

(Richard Jefferies)

visualization

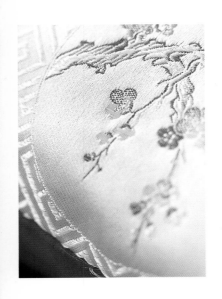

Visualization exercises, or meditations using the active imagination, are not only beneficial for relaxation. Before we can become what we want to be, or acquire what we want we need to impress our desires on the unconscious and on the ether so that opportunities will arise and we will be ready to make full use of them. The following exercises will enable you to identify your short- and long-term goals, boost your self-confidence and improve your self-image through the use of creative visualization techniques. There are also exercises designed to help you to begin exploring your inner state, to create an inner sanctuary and to seek guidance from your 'Higher Self'.

what is visualization?

'Contact with the unconscious is made through the imagination, but the images are not a product of the imagination.' (Anon)

One of the most common difficulties that I have encountered when teaching meditation is the number of people who are convinced that they cannot visualize. These days we tend to use our intellect far more than our imagination, or intuition, and so we frequently find it easier to focus on a physical object or an abstract idea rather than an image created in our mind's eye. We think through our problems and rationalize everything until there is little mystery left in life and everything that remains unexplained is dismissed because it cannot be proven to exist.

However, at the heart of the esoteric traditions of both East and West is the belief that our physical world is an illusion behind which exists a 'Greater Reality'. It is difficult for most of us to accept this because everything in the physical world seems real to our five senses. We can touch, taste, smell, see or hear everything with the exception of fresh air and electricity which we know to be real from observing their physical effects. And yet science has only recently proven the existence of dark matter, particles that are so tiny that they pass through the Earth in an unceasing stream without us being aware of them.

Once we accept that there is no solid matter as we perceive it, that matter is really only energy moving at such a low frequency that it is given the illusion of form, then we are nearer to accepting that there are worlds within worlds existing at subatomic levels where our spirit is thought to have its reality. The key to this inner dimension is the imagination, for the imagination is the medium through which we focus our mental energy to create our own happiness or hardship in this world, and our own heaven and hell in the next.

THE SCOPE OF VISUALIZATIONS

Affirmations, mindfulness and the other techniques that I have introduced you to all have their benefits, but visualizations are almost limitless in how they can be used. They can attract whatever you want in life by clearing negative conditioning that may have 'programmed' you to believe that you were inferior to others, that you must suffer in life, or that it is 'wrong' to be wealthy, for example. They can help your mind to heal your body by channelling universal energy to revitalize the affected cells and strengthen the immune system. Visualizations can also bring about communication with your 'Higher Self' for the purposes of guidance and personal growth.

HOW VISUALIZATIONS WORK

Visualizations work by using the symbols and imagery which constitute the language of the subconscious. To achieve a particular end you need to programme your subconscious by placing the appropriate image in your mind's eye. In these meditations you can then either control the scene or let the events unfold under their own momentum. Another technique is to allow images to arise spontaneously from the subconscious which can be analysed after you have returned to waking consciousness. Whatever form of meditation you practise it is important that you develop your imagination, and that you persist in this even if you find it difficult at first.

Right: We can learn a lot about ourselves and our state of mind by analysing the symbolic imagery in a visualization.

'Imagination is more important

than knowledge.' (Albert Einstein)

the first steps
in visualization

The following exercises will help you to get started in developing your powers to visualize. They can be done either sitting in a chair or lying down.

Exercise: How to visualize

This is a basic exercise to get you used to the visualization process.

Get into your chosen position. Close your eyes, breathe naturally and relax. Visualize your immediate surroundings, picturing every object in the room as vividly and in as much detail as you can.

Next, imagine leaving the room and passing slowly through the building until you reach the front door noting everything as you go. Leave the building and walk around the neighbourhood. A walk around the block and back is sufficient for the initial excursions.

Visualize your tour with full sensory perception. Can you feel the breeze on your face, the contours of the ground, the warmth or chill in the air? Listen to the sounds that you normally take for granted. When you are ready, return the way you came. Do not rush but retrace your steps in detail. Then sense the weight of your body on the chair or bed and slowly open your eyes.

Exercise: The nightly review

This exercise is excellent for sharpening visual recall and disciplining your mind to follow a linear story. It is also very useful if you have trouble falling asleep.

Every night before you go to sleep, close your eyes and recall the events of the day in reverse order, from that evening back to when you awoke that morning. If you fall asleep before you reach the end, do not worry, you probably need the rest.

Do not simply catalogue the events, but re-run them and visualize them in as much detail as you can. Sharpen your psychic senses and try to get a real sense of the atmosphere, sounds, smells, physical sensations and tastes.

Try to cultivate a sense of detachment so that you do not take everything personally, but rather accept these things as having been experienced by the body that you are inhabiting. Then let go and visualize a stream of images like a roll of movie film disappearing into the night sky to become part of the Akashic Records, or 'world memory'. This day is now part of the past. You cannot relive it. Let it go and affirm that tomorrow you will live every moment for the present.

Exercise: The corridor

This is a good exercise again to do at night as it really helps you to relax.

Close your eyes and visualize yourself standing at one end of a long corridor. Now see the word 'calm' appearing in front of you in any form or colour that you like, but keep it simple.

Hold that image firmly in focus as you send the word floating down the corridor. Do not follow it and do not allow it to disappear from view. When you have seen it safely to the end of the corridor, begin to bring it back, slowly and smoothly.

You can eventually extend the exercise when you feel you have sufficient control. You can send the word through a door at the far end of the corridor where it dissolves into a pool of warm water. After sending a number of suggestions into the pool you can follow them there and imagine immersing yourself in a calming, refreshing bath. You may have fallen asleep; otherwise slowly open your eyes.

'To perceive a distant reality as real is the function of imagination. The words "perception" and "imagination" become interchangeable on this level.' (Colin Wilson)

heal your life

Creative visualization is becoming an increasingly popular form of meditation with Westerners who find the traditional 'empty vessel' techniques of the East too abstract and who want a form of meditation that will help them to resolve a specific problem, or attain a particular goal in their life. It evolved from the ancient practice of guided inner exploration known as Pathworking, developed by the Kabbalists and occultists of the Western esoteric tradition, and was renamed Creative Imagination when adapted by the Swiss psychologist Carl Jung (1875–1961) who used it to help his patients probe the archetypal realms of the Collective Unconscious.

Now a simplified version of Jung's methods is being promoted as the ideal self-help technique by a generation of New Age Personal Growth gurus whose positive philosophy and practical exercises are enforced with affirmations. Together these techniques clear whatever negative conditioning may be preventing an individual from achieving their potential so that the subconscious mind can be reprogrammed with images of the life that they would like to live.

ACHIEVING SUCCESS WITH VISUALIZATION

For creative visualization to be effective you need to have a strong desire to achieve something and not simply be curious, for example, to know what it might be like to drive a fast car or have your boss's job. Such idle daydreams come from the ego without any thought for the responsibilities attached to them, and as such are more likely to be a curse rather than a blessing. The ideal subject for a visualization is something for which you have a strong and consistent yearning, that you feel is rightfully yours and that you strongly believe you are capable of achieving, given the opportunity. Creative visualization will create that opportunity, but it will always be up to you whether you take it and make of it what you originally imagined.

You also need to be willing to accept what you attract. Some people are actually frightened of success because they doubt that they can cope with it, that they are incapable of commitment, or that they are not deserving of its rewards. So they are constantly in pursuit of something that they subconsciously hope they will never obtain and to ensure that they never obtain it they frequently undermine their own efforts by deliberately missing important appointments or provoking those that they wish to impress.

So, if you want visualizations to work for you, be honest with yourself. In meditation ask your guide if you really want this particular thing and envisage the consequences if your wish is granted.

Another essential prerequisite states that your aim should be clearly defined. Asking for a 'better job' and limiting your visualization to a scene in which you see yourself lounging behind a big desk, or buying an expensive new car, will not send the right message to the subconscious. You might win a new car with the road tax bills and running expenses that go with it, or you might find yourself assigned to a new office with nothing to do all day, but you will not be offered more satisfying and challenging work unless you send direct signals to the subconscious.

However, it is also not a good idea to go into too much detail as you may be blocking what is right for you by insisting that it comes in a particular package. Ask most

people to describe their ideal partner or job and it is unlikely to offer the kind of challenge that they really need. What we think we want in our normal waking state is what the ego wants to satisfy its immediate and transient desires. But the basis of our personality, the 'Higher Self', knows what it needs to experience in this lifetime for its long-term development and it will invariably be greater than anything that you could have imagined yourself.

It is particularly important that you do not put faces to a partner, child or friend that you might be hoping to attract into your life. Again, your 'Higher Self' knows who is right for you to meet in order that you can both learn the lessons that you need to learn in this life. It will interfere with your own chosen life pattern if you try to impose a personality upon the subconscious. Instead be open and willing to accept whoever the Universe (the divine source) sends. In the case of a prospective partner or friend you will still have the free will to commit yourself to that relationship or not, as you see fit.

To ensure that you are open to whatever is right for you use this affirmation, or words of your own choice, while you are picturing a particular scene and just before returning to waking consciousness. 'Whatever is right for me is now manifesting in the Universe for the highest good of all concerned.'

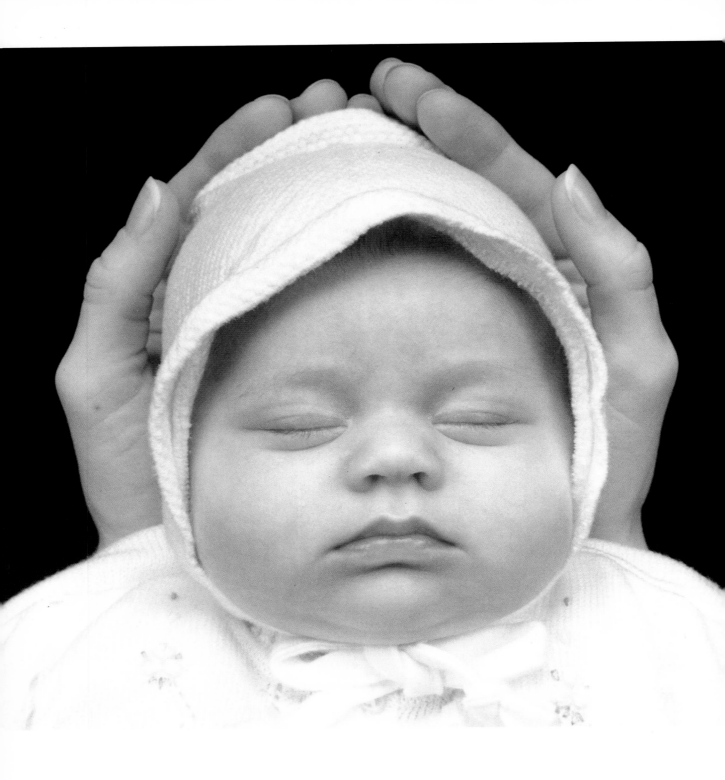

KEY VISUALIZATION MEDITATION

Exercise: The universal child

Remember before you start that to become what you want to be, you have to accept what you are.

Get into your chosen position (see pages 30–33). Close your eyes, focus on your breathing (see pages 34–35) and establish a steady rhythm. When you feel sufficiently relaxed, visualize a cluster of stars in the night sky. The more spectacular and awe-inspiring it is the better. Try to recall one of the shots of deep space taken by the Hubble telescope which are full of colour and light against the infinite blackness of space.

Now choose a tiny speck of light in the far distance and watch as it grows in size and intensity. See the particles of light and matter in the cloud of stars begin to fuse together until they form what appears to be a pair of giant hands. As you look you can see that the hands are cradling a baby – a smiling, laughing, loving baby.

This baby is you. Not the physical personality who adopted the ways of the world and is now burdened with whatever problems you had earlier today or yesterday, but the real you, the inner child, the universal child that cannot die and for whom pain, frustration, loneliness, anger and all other negative emotions have no meaning.

This child was created out of this eternal fusion of light and darkness, emptiness and energy, force and form for a purpose. That purpose was to love and to be loved. And no other reason.

If you wish you can follow this child as it is given in trust to its human parents and sense the pleasure that they share. If it has not experienced the love that it expected, or if it found for some reason that its love was not returned, understand that it is no fault of the child. It remains the highest creative expression of a loving and bountiful Universe and its one obligation is to show its love in the present, unconditionally. Not to prove its superiority over the other children, nor to amass material possessions, but to love and be loved. Nothing less.

Allow the images to take their natural course and when you feel that it is right to end the meditation, slowly return to waking consciousness.

'Happiness and spiritual growth are connected. Being peaceful and being happy form the most important foundation of spiritual practice. Then the practice goes by itself.'

(Mother Meera)

building the future

The following exercise is deceptively simple, but surprisingly effective. Use it every time that you feel anxious about the future or begin to doubt your abilities. You can also use it periodically to top up your self-confidence. If you do so, you will find that your confidence and self-esteem will steadily increase until your anxieties about the present or future go away completely.

Exercise: Boosting self-confidence

Get into your chosen position (see pages 30–33). Close your eyes, breathe naturally (see pages 34–35) and sink into a deep state of relaxation.

Think back to your earliest memories of childhood, to a time when you achieved something that surprised you and made you feel happy. Perhaps it was a physical feat, such as jumping over something that had seemed impossible for you at that age, or finding your first friend, or being brave when you went to nursery school for the first time. Our memories of childhood are usually vague, but everyone can remember something significant from their early years if they think hard enough. Trust that something will come to the surface and it will, for everything that you have done and everything that you have said has been imprinted on the subconscious. The important thing is that it should be something that pleased you, not necessarily something for which you received approval.

When you have a scene in mind, scan it for details. Take in as much of the sounds, smells and tastes as you possibly can. If you feel yourself becoming emotional, let the feelings flow because it is obviously something that needs to be expressed and cleared.

Now scan forward slowly to another incident in your childhood when you made another step forward in understanding, or proved your physical ability. Perhaps it was learning to swim or ride a bike. Can you remember if you were anxious about doing this, or maybe you doubted your ability. Can you also recall the feeling when you succeeded?

Continue like this through school, further education, your first job, relationships, setting up home and other incidents to the present moment. Let the images come to you naturally and then, when you are ready, come back to waking consciousness.

FUTURE MEDITATIONS

In any later meditations you may wish to concentrate on one particular aspect or period of your life, but initially you need to appreciate all your achievements that you now take for granted. We tend to measure our success in terms of material possessions, academic qualifications, social status or career record, but it is the small steps that we make every day that contribute to our inner growth, awareness and understanding.

We also tend to let our present difficulties obscure our past achievements with the result that temporary setbacks can make a serious dent in our self-confidence. Recalling past successes in this way is a form of mindfulness meditation (see page 38), which has a cumulative effect creating a positive and balanced self-image.

Exercise: Acknowledging your achievements

You can use this as a separate meditation, or as an extension of the previous one. If starting afresh, relax as in the previous exercise, then start to visualize doing whatever you would like to do if you had the time, money and opportunity to do whatever you wanted. Indulge your fantasy because it may reveal that what you subconsciously desire is not actually unobtainable at all. Often our dreams of unlimited wealth and success hide modest aspirations such as having more time for ourselves, the courage to act spontaneously or the need for new surroundings. Let the images flow naturally and then, when it feels right, come back to waking consciousness.

LIMITLESS ASPIRATIONS

There are no limitations to what you can attract, only your willingness to accept what is possible. If your reward is something simple that you can enjoy now, then do it. You will feel better for having treated yourself and you will attract more good fortune into your life by acting in anticipation of the promise of more to come. But if you are frightened of acting, justifying your reluctance to take risks by imagining that you are being prudent and sensible, then you are, in effect, reinforcing your fear on your subconscious. If you deny yourself something that you really want and can afford, then you are telling yourself that when that money is gone there will be no more. Of course if you sincerely believe that, then there will not be any more.

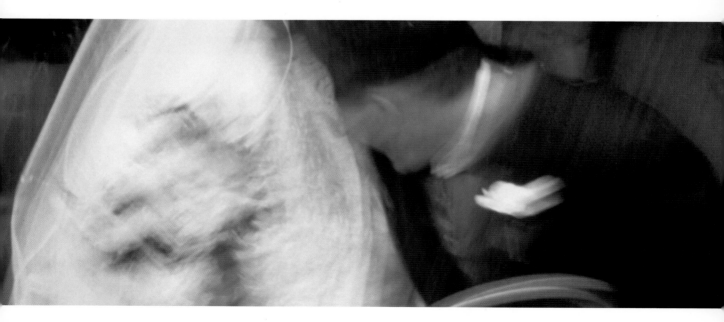

improving your
self-image

An unfortunate habit that many of us indulge in from time to time involves comparing ourselves to others. It is almost certain to result in disappointment for the simple reason that everybody is unique, possessing qualities and failings in unequal measure, according to what they have experienced in previous lives and what they need to learn in this incarnation. The Buddhist philosophy states that instead of considering ourselves as competing individuals we should be refining our true nature so that it can reflect this unique side of us without distortion.

But to do this we first need to free ourselves from the false image that we have of ourselves which goes no deeper than the physical shell, and which is coloured by the comments and conditioning on which our ego depends for its reality.

Exercise: Self-portrait

Get into your chosen position (see pages 30–33). Close your eyes, and relax into a regular rhythm of breathing (see pages 34–35). Visualize yourself in an art gallery standing before a full-length portrait of yourself as you were when you were really happy.

Take a long look at yourself and consider what you see in those eyes, in the facial features and in the way that you hold yourself. What type of character has the artist captured?

Now you hear approaching footsteps. A small crowd of friends, family members and past acquaintances have come to admire your portrait and tell you why they love or respect you. There is no need to be self-conscious or to display false modesty. In this dimension everyone speaks the truth. This occasion is not the place for criticism, but for appreciation and deserving praise. This is not an empty gesture, but a demonstration of genuine affection.

See each person in turn as they approach the portrait and listen as they declare your qualities to the group. You may be surprised by what they reveal. Others often admire us for qualities that we may take for granted.

When everyone has spoken their piece take another long look at the portrait. Has it changed? If so, in what way? In the light of what has been said by your friends and family do you think that you have been too self-critical in the past? Have you been driving yourself too hard rather than treating yourself as you would your best friend?

Now consider, if all these people love you for the reasons that they have stated, then how can you not love yourself?

Look at the portrait for the last time and in your own words affirm that you are a loving, intelligent, creative person. Find other thoughts that come to mind. Use whatever attributes you can recall other people saying. Then, when you have finished, gradually return to waking consciousness.

APPRECIATING YOUR LIFE

As an adjunct to this exercise and the meditation on the previous page it is a good idea to put yourself into a meditative mood a couple of times a week and make a mental inventory of all those things in your life which give you pleasure. These can range from your state of health or your sense of humour to the companionship of your friends or even possessions which you appreciate.

Some people feel guilty about having a wealth of possessions and material comforts, but it is important to accept what the universe has provided and also to accept that we live in an abundant world where there is plenty of everything for everybody. Putting conditions or limitations on your happiness and success does not help those who have less. It simply restricts your powers to manifest what you want and have the right to have in your own life.

Whether you consider these 'blessings' to be gifts from God, symbols of good fortune or the rewards of hard work is not important. What you are doing by recalling these things to mind is reinforcing your image of yourself as a healthy, happy and attractive personality with the ability to attract what you want into your life. Enjoy it.

'Whatever you do, don't shut off your pain; accept your pain and remain vulnerable. However desperate you become, accept your pain as it is, because it is in fact trying to hand you a priceless gift: the chance of discovering, through spiritual practice, what lies behind sorrow.' (Sogyal Rinpoche)

setting yourself goals

'What you are is what you

have done, what you will

be is what you do now.'

(The Buddha)

Creative visualization can also be used to clarify your aims in life and find out what is really important to you at a particular point in your life.

The American personal growth guru Shakti Gawain, author of *Creative Visualisation* and *Living in the Light*, gives several examples of how to do so, including the making of a 'wish list' and visualizing an ideal scene.

In the former all you have to do is draw up a list of things that you want to achieve under the appropriate headings. These include Work/Career, Money, Lifestyle/Possessions, Relationships, Creative Self-Expression, Leisure/Travel and Personal Growth/Education.

If, for example, you want a more satisfying job, write a brief and unambiguous sentence under the heading 'Work/Career' along the lines of 'I want a more satisfying and better-paid job which will be right for me in every respect, which will not require me to commute or move away from here and which will still leave me time for my family'. If you are not specific you may be offered more

satisfying work but it might require you to move to the other end of the country and to work longer hours. Of course you always have the free will to refuse the offer, but if you are desperate for work you may feel obliged to take it.

ACHIEVING YOUR GOALS

I can personally vouch for the efficacy of this exercise as I received the new car, work, possessions and exact income that I had specified within a year of doing the exercise. I also went abroad on a spiritual pilgrimage which I probably would not have had the courage or opportunity to do had I not expressed that subconscious longing in my list. The only thing I did not do was to learn a foreign language because I simply did not have the time after doing the extra work that had come my way!

Exercises of this nature may not appear to be meditations in the traditional sense, but they require a similar degree of heightened concentration and awareness that will bring secret hopes to the surface. We all think we know what we want to ensure our happiness, but until we focus our minds in this way we tend to drift through life with only a vague idea of what we are aiming for and put our trust in fate. Without a clear idea of what we want in our lives we will not be able to create it, because there will be no goal towards which we can channel our mental energy.

Exercise: Creating your ideal world

Write down the first of the seven categories listed on page 84 at the top of a large blank piece of paper, then get into your chosen position (see pages 30–33). Close your eyes, breathe naturally (see pages 34–35) and meditate on that theme, allowing your ideal scene to form in its own time. It is the quality of your life that you are looking to improve, so in the first meditation on the theme of Work/Career it is important to see yourself being relaxed and pleased with your work, rather than simply being successful. Do not limit yourself; be generous. In freeing your imagination in this way you could be surprised to discover aims and ideas of which you were previously unaware.

When you have finished your meditation, gradually return to waking consciousness and write down everything that you can remember. Then do the same with the second category until you have a paragraph or two for each of the seven scenes.

SETTING TIME LIMITS

Now read through what you have written down and choose ten specific goals that you can identify from the descriptions. Then select those which you can imagine achieving over the course of the next five years and write these down in a new list under the heading 'Five-year Goals'.

Do the same again for those which seem to be realistic aims for the coming year, and finally list those which you feel comfortable aiming to fulfil within the next six months.

Clarifying your short-term goals in this way will help you to identify the stages that you need in order to achieve your long-term ambitions, so that they do not remain mere fantasies. But do not aim too high or you will soon lose heart if you fail to fulfil the short-term steps. Above all, keep them simple and choose goals that will make you feel great when you succeed, rather than choosing things that you feel you ought to achieve to fulfil someone else's expectations.

seeking help

The following exercise uses the symbol of a kite which is very good to work with in a visualization. The kite has associations with the wonder and carefree days of childhood and it also represents something that is nominally free but still under control. Used as an alternative to prayer it develops trust in the universe to provide help, and it also acts as an emotional release as the person is encouraged to gradually let go of their inner anxieties.

Exercise: The kite

Get into your chosen position (see pages 31–33). Close your eyes, and breathe naturally (see pages 34–35), then when you feel sufficiently relaxed start visualizing yourself on a windswept hillside. Look down on the rolling fields, hills and winding country lanes below. Feel the freshening wind in your hair and the warmth of the sun on your face. Now see yourself kicking off your shoes and taking off your socks to sense the soft grass under your feet.

Beside you on the grass is a kite made to your own design. Is it the traditional diamond shape or in the form of an animal, a bird or a geometrical shape? Is it large or small? What colour is it? What material is it made from? Wrapped around the tail of the kite are a number of bows which you are going to unravel one at a time.

Unravel the first bow. It might be larger or smaller than you expected, but it will be the right size for your needs. Now write your name and the first thing that comes into your mind. It might be a single word, a sentence or a short list of words and phrases. It might even come in the form of a symbol. When your mind is silent again re-tie the bow.

Unravel the next bow and write the word 'Love', followed by the first thing that comes into your mind. When you are finished re-tie the bow.

Unravel the third bow, write the word 'Worry', following it with the first thing that comes into your mind.

Unravel the fourth bow and write the word 'Hope'. Again write whatever next comes into your mind and then re-tie the bow.

Now unravel the fifth and final bow and write whatever is concerning you at the moment that you would like to be resolved or for which you require some guidance. Add anything you want to aid its journey out into the etheric world, such as a prayer or a short message. You could write 'with love', an entreatment that your message is heeded, or even address it 'to whom it may concern'. Draw a heart around it if you like, or attach something that is significant such as a flower or a lock of your own hair, or that of a person that you might be concerned for. Do not try to analyse your actions; just do whatever comes naturally and spontaneously to mind.

Now reel out the string of the kite and watch it as it soars into the sky. Keep a tight rein on it. Play the line and watch as it weaves through the clouds. Keep it in view as you lengthen the line and as you do so sense your attachment to the kite lessening. Reel it in to reinforce your control over it, then gradually let the line slip through your fingers as you prepare to cast your concerns into the clouds. Do you feel ready to let go of the string?

Release it and watch as the kite disappears into the clouds. Trust that your thoughts and feelings will be acted upon by the 'Universal Force' for the highest good of all concerned. When you feel ready, gradually return to waking consciousness by counting down from ten to one.

As soon as you can, record the messages that you received in your journal. Do not forget to make a description of the kite for further analysis.

the desert island

'The point of power is always in the present moment.' (Louise L. Hay)

Exercise: The desert island

Get into your chosen position (see pages 30–33). Close your eyes, breathe naturally (see pages 34–35), and when you feel suitably relaxed begin to visualize yourself sitting under a palm tree in swimwear at sunrise on a deserted beach on an idyllic desert island.

Placed beside you are your everyday clothes and the suitcase that you brought with you containing everything that you believe is of value to you and which you feel you cannot do without in your daily life. Open the case and examine its contents. Here are the essential items you have brought from work and from home. How significant do these seem to you now that you are so far away from your office, school or home? Perhaps there is something you feel you could discard, something that has been a burden and that you would not miss if you returned without it? If so, take it out and bury it in the sand. Then think no more about it.

Now you turn to watch the sun rise; its rays are turning the ocean flaming red and orange but it is not too hot for you at this early hour of the day, sitting in the shade of the palm tree.

As the sun climbs in the sky the ocean looks clear and icy blue in colour. You feel drawn to walk to the water's edge. Imagine yourself stretching and standing up leaving behind all your stress and cares. Feel the fine white sand under your feet and between your toes as you wiggle them for the sheer sense of playfulness you get with knowing that you have escaped all of your cares.

Smell the fresh sea air and feel the breeze blowing through your hair and touching your body. Hear the sound of gulls circling in the sky above you and the distant call of exotic parrots and other birds in the jungle behind you.

Walk down to the seashore, and then go along the beach stopping occasionally to bend down and look at the shells that have been washed up on the shore. Pick up a shell that attracts you and turn it over in your hand. Run your fingers over its contours and feel the texture of its surface.

The water looks cool and inviting. You wade in and find it pleasantly warm. You can still feel the sand between your toes but now you also feel the warmth of the water lapping against your legs.

A small brightly coloured fish swims by. You wade out a little further where you can see the coral under the surface of the sparkling water. Another exotic-coloured fish swims up to you and circles round you before swimming away. Perhaps you feel like swimming. Even if you cannot swim, immerse yourself in the clear refreshing water and feel all your anxieties being washed away.

When you feel ready, begin to wade back to the shore. On reaching the beach, walk up to the palm tree and retrieve your everyday clothes. Take another look in your suitcase and consider its contents. Is there anything else that you now feel you could discard? Take a long hard look and see if you are carrying anything that is of little real value or use to you.

Now dress yourself and prepare to return to waking consciousness, but before you do so tell yourself that you will retain the sense of this revitalizing experience for the rest of the day.

Now focus again on your breathing. Become aware of your surroundings and the weight of your body sitting in the chair, and slowly open your eyes.

secret hopes and aspirations

Above and right: **The details of a house and its surroundings can reveal a great deal about the occupant's inner state and aspirations.**

TIP

Many people say that they enjoy meditation because they can drift off. But drifting off and losing the focus of the exercise is not meditating.

The key to meditation is focusing with detachment, being hyper-aware and not spaced out. Drifting off on your own fantasy during a guided visualization such as this one, is the equivalent of taking a much needed holiday to the Bahamas and then falling asleep on the beach.

If you need proof that visualizations are much more than sophisticated daydreams then this exercise should give it to you. This particular version is my adaptation of an inner exploration which has been used from ancient times to the present day. Its effectiveness in teasing out those secret hopes and concerns that lie just beneath the surface of your consciousness will be evident on your first attempt. However, with regular practice the details will change to reflect your inner state. I have to admit that I have used this exercise to 'hook' new students at taster sessions and that it has never failed to stimulate their interest in meditation.

Exercise: House of the spirit

Get into your chosen position (see pages 30–33). Close your eyes, breathe naturally (see pages 34–35), and when you feel sufficiently relaxed begin to visualize a rural landscape with a house in the distance. Note the weather and details of whatever lies between you and the house. Let the images arise spontaneously. Do not try to change them into what you would like to see instead, and do not be tempted to analyse them now.

Begin to walk towards the house. Again note the details of the terrain. Is it difficult to cross? Is it overgrown or cultivated? Do you find yourself in a field of flowers or a bleak, windswept scrubland with nettles? Are there obstacles and, if so, do you overcome them easily?

You are now standing at the boundary of the property. Does it have a wall and, if so, is it high or low? Is there a door or gate in the wall and what condition is it in? Beyond the gate is there a garden, a paved area or a yard strewn with rubble? If there is a garden, then note if it is well tended or if it is overgrown.

Now you are at the front door. What type of door is it and is it easy to open? Once inside you are faced with stairs leading to the first floor. Walk up the stairs and enter the room that faces you. Take time to absorb every detail of the furnishings and particularly the painting that is on the far wall.

There are also a desk and a chair by the window. Take a look out of the window. What do you see? Now make yourself comfortable in the chair and open the envelope that you will find on the desk with your name on it. Read the letter and note its contents carefully. What exactly does it say? It may be valuable advice on a subject that has been concerning you recently.

In return for this advice you take something from your pocket and put it in the envelope before placing it back on the desk. Now leave the room and return the way you came, noting any changes to the house and its surroundings as you do so.

When you feel ready, slowly return to waking consciousness by counting down from ten to one. Before you forget it, write down everything you can remember in your journal.

ANALYSING WHAT YOU SAW

Using your common sense and a good dictionary of symbols will help you to analyse whatever you saw, but the following notes will serve as a guide to get you started. As you become more experienced in exploring your psyche you will be able to trust your intuition more so that the significance of the symbolism becomes clearer. Your meditations will then become an ever more valuable source of insight into your attitudes and what is happening to you currently.

The surrounding landscape in the exercise represents your attitude to your current circumstances. Heavy skies and difficult terrain suggests that you anticipate problems and that you see them as an unfair hindrance to your ambitions.

Walls and gates

The wall symbolizes your resistance to inner guidance. If there is no wall or the wall is too low then it indicates that you have already demonstrated a willingness to trust your own intuition.

The gate or door in the wall is symbolic of the connection between the conscious mind and the subconscious. The size of the entrance and the ease with which you entered indicates your current ability to enter this altered state of consciousness.

The area beyond the door or gate symbolizes your present state of mind. A garden that is overgrown with weeds represents worries and unresolved matters that need to be dealt with. A rubble-strewn yard might symbolize a fear that whatever you undertake will fail, even if there is no rational reason for this belief. It can also represent a lot of matters that are unresolved and are preventing you from moving forward.

Entering the house

The front door of the house represents your attitude to life, the ease with which you are prepared to try new things and the manner in which you expect to be received by other people.

The house itself represents your psyche. If it is old-fashioned but in good decorative order, then you are rather conservative by nature and concerned with personal comfort. If it is bright, spacious and of modern design then you are more forward-looking, open to new ideas and generally adventurous.

The staircase is symbolic of your family life. Narrow or steep steps indicate what you perceive to be insurmountable problems, while a spiral staircase suggests that you feel the need to avoid difficult situations at home.

The view from the window in the room on the first floor symbolizes your dreams. These might be unfulfilled ambitions, childhood memories, hopes for the future, or what you insist on seeing as lost opportunities. Whatever they signify, if you find yourself becoming emotional do not try to suppress it. Let it flow and move on. The next time you look through the window you should be pleasantly surprised.

The room's contents

The painting could be either a self-portrait or a symbol of something of great significance for you at this present time. If it is a self-portrait it might appear in the image of your true nature, which will be ageless, loving and compassionate. However, it might also appear in a form that reveals what you are feeling deep down inside – emotions that are hidden from your conscious self and the world at large. Do not be surprised if it does not look like you at all, but has an air of strange familiarity. It could be one of your previous incarnations!

The letter is a message from your 'Higher Self' and the object that you put into the envelope can be either something that you secretly wish to unburden yourself of or a gift to that inner personality. The significance of the object should become clear if you meditate upon it. Many people do not see anything written on the letter when they meditate, but it frequently comes to them in the form of an inspired idea during their sleep later that same night.

If you have unburdened yourself of something or have benefited from making this journey, then the surroundings should change accordingly as you retrace your steps.

the inner sanctuary

'I am relaxed and centred. I have plenty of time for everything.'

(Affirmation, anon)

Every person exists on several levels of reality simultaneously – the physical, emotional, mental and spiritual realms. When we meditate, we raise our awareness of these levels as we rise in consciousness from the purely physical to examine our feelings and then our thoughts, and, ultimately, expand our consciousness beyond the physical senses.

It is therefore important that, after creating 'sacred space' in which to work on the physical plane, that we do the same on the inner planes where the process of transformation can continue. To do this we can use a visualization to create a garden where we can seek sanctuary whenever we need to withdraw momentarily from the world. Many people think that this is merely exercising the imagination, but, just as our soul exists in a dimension that we are rarely conscious of, so the garden will have its reality in the inner realm as a 'thought form', brought into existence by you with each successive meditation.

THE SYMBOLIC GARDEN

The garden is an archetypal image common to many spiritual traditions which might otherwise appear incompatible on the surface. The Kabbalah, for example, envisages existence as a series of four interpenetrating worlds of increasing refinement in which the psychological realm is symbolized as a pastoral paradise. This was mythologized in the Old Testament as the Garden of Eden and is the source of the Christian concept of Heaven. It is no coincidence that the Koran (the sacred book of Islam) also describes the realms beyond our own as four Gardens of Paradise, for the Islamic mystics shared the same image of the structure of existence.

We should also not be surprised that the same imagery recurs in innumerable modern accounts of near-death experiences described by ordinary individuals with no particular religious conviction, for the garden is a universal symbol of the sacred space in which the soul has its reality.

Exercise: The walled garden

Make yourself comfortable and get into your chosen position. Close your eyes and breathe naturally, relaxing into a regular rhythm. When you feel ready, visualize yourself standing before the entrance to a walled garden; perhaps it is a door covered with vines or an iron gate through which you can glimpse the garden just beyond.

Enter the garden and look around you. What are your first impressions? Is it a rambling cottage garden or laid out in a neat, formal design? Is it well kept or neglected? Are there weeds and thistles among the flowers? Are there fruit trees or vegetables?

Can you smell the scent of the flowers? Can you hear the droning of bees or the sweet singing of birds? Can you feel the breeze on your face? Can you get a sense of what the flowers feel like to the touch? Pick up a handful of soil. Is it dry and lifeless or friable and rich in nutrients? Is it sticky and clay-like?

Look at the sky. Is it overcast or clear? What season is it? Look at the wall that encloses the garden. Is it low, head-height or unusually high and imposing? Are there any special features such as a sundial, a raised bed of herbs or a pond?

Is there somewhere you can sit and contemplate your surroundings or think over a problem? If not, now is the time to create one. You might also wish to get started on tidying up the flower beds, sweeping the paths, cutting the grass, pruning dead flower heads and so on. But this is not work. It requires no effort, only the will to make your vision a reality and create a sanctuary in a world beyond your imagination.

It is here that you can invite your guide to join you whenever you need help or advice and you can be confident that you will receive it. But now it is time to return slowly to waking consciousness, bringing the peace of this place with you back into the 'real world'. Record all your impressions in your journal.

the path to
inner peace

This section offers advanced techniques to bring variety and greater depth to your practice, and for safely probing deeper into the psyche. After a look at the value of mantras and music and an outline describing how to incorporate them into your routine there is a description of the relationship between the chakras of the Hindu tradition and the sephiroth of the Kabbalistic system.

Exercises include the 'Middle Pillar' visualisation for clearing and centring the chakras, a 'Pathworking' for exploring a specific area of the psyche and a method for exploring past lives.

mantras for meditation

MANTRAS

From the earliest times monks and mystics have used mantras and chants to induce a trance-like state. Many cultures and traditions, including the ancient Egyptians, adhered to the belief that existence itself was created by sound (a concept adopted by the early Christians who conceived of 'The Word' as the manifest expression of God). Even today certain sounds are held to be sacred in the Hindu and Vedic traditions, while Jewish law forbids the name of God to be spoken in the belief that it can facilitate the act of creation (a belief which gave rise to the 'words of power' venerated by the medieval magicians).

It was not until the 1960s that the connection between sound and physical form was proven scientifically by Hans Jenny. He discovered that specific sounds produced consistent, symmetrical patterns that bore a striking resemblance to certain Tibetan mandalas, which are symbolic images of universal harmony used in meditation. The Swiss psychologist, Carl Jung, had earlier concluded that the power of mandalas is due to the fact that they represent stages in the integration of the psyche.

STILLING THE MIND

It is thought that every living organism emits its own unique vibration which is translated in the strength and colours of the aura. For that reason those who practise Transcendental Meditation (TM) (see pages 20–21) are given a personal mantra which is an expression of their unique vibration. However, TM is an exception and has been criticised for creating an atmosphere of exclusivity which is contrary to the principles of spiritual practice. The majority of mantras are simply words or phrases

Above: **Carl Jung concluded that the power of mandalas (symbolic images of universal harmony) reflect stages of our inner evolution.**

designed to still the mind and can be freely used by anyone. One of the most commonly used chants is the Buddhist benediction '*Aum mani padme hum*', which roughly translates as '*Hail to the jewel in the lotus*', an acknowledgement of the Buddha nature that is present in us all.

The chanting of mantras remains a central practice in Buddhist meditation where the sounds themselves have a mystical significance. For example, 'O' is considered to be the sound of unity and perfection, 'U' represents the descent of spirit into matter, 'A' expresses intellect and communication, 'H' is the sound of the breath and therefore of life, while 'M' is the sound between the unity of spirit and the duality of matter.

In the Tibetan tradition the three primary sounds on which most mantras are based are seen as expressions of the mind, body and soken word. 'OM' is the transcendent Universal Unity, 'AH' is the fully realized human being and 'HUM' is the individual.

PRACTISING MANTRAS IN THE WEST

Many Western meditation groups introduce mantras so that students can experience the effects for themselves. However, few Westerners adopt the practice as part of their regular routine because they feel self-conscious or are uncomfortable with repeating a phrase in a language that they do not understand.

But every tradition has suitable phrases that can be freely adopted, and for those who do not subscribe to a particular faith or philosophy the chanting of one's own name is said to be equally effective. Alternatively, if you have a particular goal in mind, such as stopping smoking or increasing your self-confidence, you can use a suitable affirmation which the cyclic chanting will help to imprint in your subconscious. Otherwise a single word such as 'Relax' is sufficient to induce a feeling of calm prior to an important meeting or at the end of a busy day.

Exercise: Using mantras

Whatever word or phrase you choose as your mantra to lead you into meditation, it will only be effective if you intone it in the following way.

Get into your chosen position. Take as deep a breath as you can, then let the air out as slowly and evenly as you can while chanting your chosen phrase. The sound should be said as loud and as clearly as possible so that its vibration creates sympathetic resonance in your chest.

Endeavour to create a continuous loop so that the end of the phrase melts into the beginning of the next. Keep the intonation and rhythm even, synchronized with your breathing or heartbeat so that the monotony of the sound becomes hypnotic.

If you wish you can gradually reduce the volume until the chant is created in your mind. Then allow it to dissipate and immerse yourself in the ensuing stillness.

Try not to think about the meaning of the mantra but rather let it become a meaningless sound in which you are absorbed. Let the last intonation fade away naturally and gradually return to waking consciousness.

music for meditation

'Music can provide a temporary retreat from
the pains of existence.'

(Anthony Storr, 'Music and the Mind')

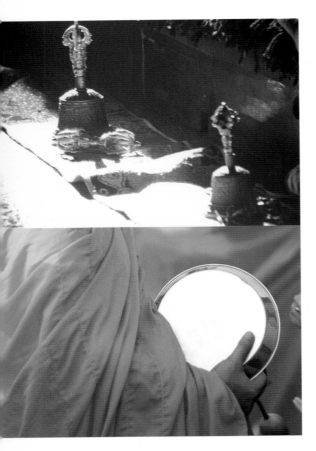

Above: Music has long been an integral
component of ritual in the Eastern
spiritual tradition.

Music has proven to be a wonderful aid to meditation,
providing a focus to help still the mind and attune it to
specific states of consciousness. In the East the use of
bells, drums, other ethnic instruments and single
sustained notes has long been an integral part of the
meditation ritual, whereas in the West it has been an
important feature of ceremonial worship, as an aid to
contemplation rather than meditation.

It was not until the 18th century that the potential
therapeutic value of music was taken seriously in the
West. Count Kayserling, a Russian envoy, was suffering
from insomnia and in desperation commissioned the
German composer Johann Sebastian Bach to write a
light piece of music to soothe his nerves. The next time
he could not sleep the Count summoned a harpsichord
player, Johann Goldberg, and asked him to play the
specially written piece of music. Within minutes the
Count fell soundly asleep.

This piece of music and subsequent compositions by
Bach, which were collectively known as the Goldberg
Variations, were the subject of scientific study in the
1970s by Dr Georgi Lozanov. The Bulgarian scientist
discovered that the opening and closing theme of each
variation induced a meditative state by slowing down the
body's biological functions. The same effect was found to
be an intrinsic characteristic of other slow movements by
composers of the Baroque period, namely Handel,
Vivaldi, Telemann and Corelli.

Now recent studies suggest that instrumental music,
particularly those movements with a constant tempo of
60 beats per minute, can be an invaluable aid in
reprogramming the subconscious mind with positive
suggestions to aid healing and achieve personal goals. It

Left: The modern practitioner of meditation can access a seemingly limitless library of suitable music and natural sounds to enhance relaxation.

appears that the steady, regular tempo and predictable harmonic progression serves to induce alpha states, which is a sense of relaxed alertness in which the brain assimilates and retains information more readily.

AUTOGENIC TRAINING

This is one particularly well-known form of complementary therapy in which visualizations are enhanced by music to achieve specific purposes, such as increasing self-confidence or inducing restful sleep. The technique was developed in the 1920s by the German psychiatrist Johannes H. Schulz who discovered that by focusing on the weight and warmth of the body his patients relaxed automatically. In this state he also found that they were more receptive to suggestions and able to overcome any resistance that had been created by long-term conditioning.

CHOOSING THE RIGHT MUSIC

The following slow movements from Johann Sebastian Bach have been found to be particularly conducive to meditation, but any piece from an opera aria to the minimalist mantras of Michael Nyman and Philip Glass can be used. When choosing a piece of music as a focus for meditation remember that the idea is to stay relaxed but alert, rather than to drift off with the music:

Largo from the Solo Harpsichord Concerto in C major.
Largo from the Solo Harpsichord Concerto in F major.
Largo from the Solo Harpsichord Concerto in G major.
Largo from the Concerto in G minor for Flute and Strings.
Largo from the Harpsichord Concerto in F minor.

As a general rule any music which has a constant pulse of 60 beats per minute will induce the relaxation response, but each piece will trigger a specific emotion or quality because its dominant tone creates a vibrational frequency which corresponds to one of the major chakras. It is no coincidence that there are eight notes in the octave (seven different notes with the eighth being a repetition of the root) and seven major chakras. When consciousness is raised to the point of the eighth chakra a person will attain union with their 'Higher Self' and a new octave of awareness unfolds.

'Music is [the] fourth dimension.'

(Sri Karunamayee)

the chakras and the sephiroth

Although the belief systems of East and West appear to express conflicting views of existence, their esoteric or hidden traditions share the same principles. For example, both the Hindu and the Jewish mystics see every human being as a microcosm, a universe in miniature, where we contain not only the elements in finite form but also the 'Divine Attributes' of the Creator. In the Hindu teachings these are symbolized by the chakras, or subtle energy centres (see also page 60), in the etheric body which regulate the circulation of vital energy.

In the Jewish mystical tradition, known as Kabbalah, (which is the basis of the Western esoteric tradition), they are symbolized as the Sephiroth, which are visualized as being multi-faceted spheres of light serving the same function. Although the Sephiroth were conceived as symbols representing abstract concepts, they can also be thought of as being specific stages on the journey to self-realization, which can be explored and experienced through creative visualization exercises known as Pathworking (see pages 106–109).

When superimposed on the human body the configuration of the Sephiroth are seen to correspond with the chakras. Our limbs represent the outer active and passive Pillars, which are the governing principles that keep the complementary attributes in balance, while the spine represents the central Pillar of Equilibrium.

The following meditation is based on an exercise devised by Israel Regardie, a founder member of the Hermetic Order of the Golden Dawn, an esoteric group predominant in Victorian England who sought direct mystical experiences by adapting the mystical practices of both East and West.

Exercise: The middle pillar

Do not be surprised if this exercise makes you emotional as it is designed to stimulate the Sephiroth and clear any emotional blocks. If you feel tearful it is best to give in to your feelings as suppressing them can sometimes lead to health problems and an increasingly negative attitude to life in general. Regular practice of this meditation will help create a feeling of being 'centred' and in control so that you are not so easily knocked off balance by things that would have upset you in the past.

Get into your chosen position. Close your eyes, and begin by focusing on your breathing. When you feel sufficiently relaxed, imagine a soft white pinpoint of light above your head and visualize it as it grows in size and intensity. This is the crown Sephirah, the source of celestial energy.

Absorb the light until it fills your head dissolving all tension and activating your third eye in the middle of your forehead between the Sephirah of Binah (Understanding) and Hokhmah (Wisdom). At this point you might feel a tickling sensation between the brows as your psychic senses are stimulated, but if you receive any spontaneous images or symbols do not be tempted to analyse them now. Stay focused on the light and leave any analysis for when you have returned to waking consciousness.

Now visualize the light being absorbed into the other Sephiroth activating these energy centres. Firstly see it being taken in by the throat which corresponds to Daat, the Sephirah representing the veil to higher knowledge. Then see it moving to the heart centre governed by the

Left: The Kabbalistic tradition of the sephiroth are akin to Hindu chakras in their formation. Each sephirah, symbolizes the active male and passive female attributes of the Creator.

Sephirah Gevurah (Judgement), Hesed (Mercy) and Tiferet (Beauty), the latter symbolizing the place of the 'Higher Self'.

Next it moves to the solar plexus centre, the realm of the emotions, governed by the Sephirah Hod (Reverberation) and Nezah (Eternity), which represent the intellect and the instincts. The light then travels to the sacral centre, the place of the 'Lower Self' or ego ruled by the Yesod (the Foundation) Sephirah.

Finally it moves to the feet, the root centre, governed by the Sephirah Malkhut (the Kingdom). This is where we are grounded in the physical realm.

See each Sephirah as a spinning crystal or whirling vortex of light. See them forming a single shaft of light energy from your crown to your feet and feel yourself 'centred', radiating light in an oval-shaped aura that illuminates the space that you are working in.

Now gradually inhale and imagine the energy rising from your feet back up into your crown until it overflows in a fountain of light cascading down your left-hand side as you exhale.

Inhale slowly again, drawing the energy up the right-hand side of your body and back through your crown and down through your body to the toes as you exhale.

Repeat this process several times until the energy is freely circulating. On your last exhalation, visualize the energy overflowing from your crown down the front of your body. As you inhale again draw it up behind you from your heels to your crown. Imagine yourself bathing in the shower of light energy as you repeat the sequence until you feel 'centred' and cleansed.

End the exercise by closing your energy centres from the top downwards, and bringing yourself back down to earth – 'grounding' yourself by stamping your feet.

clearing negative emotions

'We all cling to the past and because we cling to the past we become unavailable to the present.' (Bhagwan Shree Rajneesh)

In the Buddhist tradition there is an allegorical tale of two monks who were returning to their monastery from a pilgrimage when they came upon an old woman sitting by a fast-flowing stream. The old woman asked the monks if they could help her to cross and one of them immediately offered to carry her on his back. When he had done so he returned to find that his companion had not waited for him and was already some distance away. When he eventually caught up with him he found him to be silent and rather sullen so asked him what was causing him such pain. 'Monks are forbidden from physical contact with women', said the sullen monk. 'Indeed,' replied the first, 'but I put her down safely on the far bank an hour ago and you are still carrying her.'

We all have the tendency to burden ourselves with emotional baggage from our past, even when we know that it is impeding our future progress. The following exercise will help you to clear deeply rooted thought patterns created by painful past memories, persistent regrets or nagging resentments.

Exercise: Clearing out the past

Get into your chosen position. Close your eyes and breathe naturally, getting into a regular rhythm. When you are sufficiently relaxed visualize a remote mountain track leading to a temple a few hundred yards from where you are now standing.

For a moment stay silent and listen to the sound of the birds in the trees, the bubbling waters of a nearby brook and the distant tinkling of wind chimes hanging by the temple door. The air is thick with the scent of pine needles and mountain flowers.

You begin to walk up the track toward the temple and as you approach you can hear the sound of muted voices chanting a mantra that stirs emotions deep within you.

The primal sound invites you to go within.

You pause at the entrance and remove your shoes. The door is ajar and an elderly monk sitting just inside the entrance beckons you inside. You mount the ten wooden steps and enter the temple where the scent of incense is intoxicating.

In the half-light you see a line of Buddhist monks sitting cross-legged on either side from the door to the altar. The temple is lit by candles and the flames are steady, throwing the shadows of the monks upon the walls and illuminating the wisps of incense smoke that are curling into the rafters.

Now walk towards the altar at the far end which is decorated in a gold-coloured cloth engraved with images of Buddha. Here bowls of water and fruit adorn the altar. Perhaps you have brought an offering that you can add. If so, what is it?

You bow before the statue of the Buddha which stands behind the altar, but this is not idol worship – you are acknowledging your own Buddha nature of which the statue is a symbol.

Before you is a low stool on which there rests some sheets of paper and a pen. Sitting cross-legged before the altar you begin to write whatever regrets you may be clinging to, whatever memories bring you pain and the resentments that you may be harbouring from the past. Now is the time to soften your heart centre, express what is deeply felt but unspoken and offer these all these regrets to the purifying flame that is the light of the Buddha of compassion.

When you have finished, fold the paper into a taper and place it in the burning bowl sitting at the feet of the Buddha. Watch as the paper shrivels into ash and affirm in words of your own choosing that you are now relieved of all those things which have burdened you for too long.

Forgive yourself and accept whatever happened to you as a learning experience.

Remain seated before the altar, contemplating the symbol of your own Buddha nature and the serenity within. Know that the only thing separating you from your divine nature is your attachment to the transient things of the physical world. Let go of what you cannot control and be centred in your self. When you feel ready return to waking consciousness, count down slowly from ten to one and then open your eyes.

'Inner peace can be reached only when we practise forgiveness. Forgiveness is the letting go of the past, and is therefore the means for correcting our misperceptions.'

(Gerald Jampolsky)

pathworking

'I have always made a distinction between pictures seen in the memory of nature and visions of actual beings now existing in the inner world...mystical beings in their own world are never seen with the physical eyes.'

(Israel Regardie)

Opposite, left: The Tree of Life depicted in stained glass in the Great Synagogue, Jerusalem .

Opposite, left: The Tree of Life depicted in stained glass in the Great Synagogue, Jerusalem .

Opposite, right: The divine attributes of the creation, as symbolized by the Sephiroth on the Tree of Life.

Whenever we plan a journey by visualizing it in our minds, or when we prepare ourselves to do something difficult by imagining what it will be like, we are Pathworking at a mundane level. But these are idle daydreams which have no lasting effect on our lives, whereas Pathworking within the confines of a structured meditation can have a profound effect on us.

Pathworking and visualization are often confused, but they differ in one important respect. The former uses the imagination to open the door into other realities, whereas the latter is the process by which we can create a new reality in the physical world by first making a blueprint on the inner plane.

AN ANCIENT TRADITION

Pathworking is an ancient form of meditation where consciousness is projected into other dimensions to gain direct experience of various levels of awareness. These levels are symbolized as paths on the Kabbalistic Tree of Life, from which the practice took its name. However, the concept is not exclusive to initiates of Kabbalah (see page 18), the Jewish mystical teachings which form the foundation of the Western esoteric tradition.

Over the centuries the technique has been adopted by diverse esoteric groups and spiritual seekers who share a similar philosophy and structure of existence. More recently it has been adapted by psychotherapists to guide patients into the realms of the subconscious, although they have renamed it 'Active Imagination' in an effort to exorcise its esoteric associations.

In each case those who adopt the technique simply exchange the archetypal symbols for their own. Those with an affinity for the Arthurian legends, for example, can substitute the mythical characters of Arthur, Guinevere, Lancelot and Merlin for the traditional

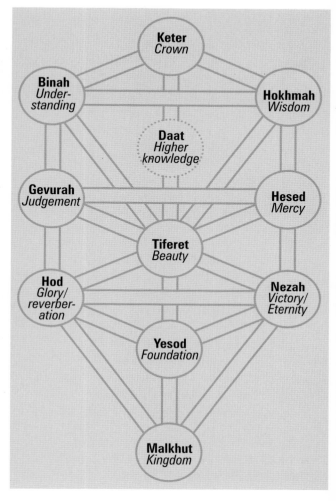

archetypes who personify the Divine Attributes on the Tree of Life, initiates of the Egyptian Mysteries put Osiris, Seth and Isis in the corresponding roles, while others have used the images shown on tarot cards. Envisaging these archetypes during a structured meditation is thought to help the initiate to explore, strengthen and integrate those aspects of their own personality.

USING THE PATHWORKING TECHNIQUE

If you choose to work with this technique there are several points worth remembering.

• Pathworking is no more dangerous than playing a fantasy role – which it resembles in certain respects – unless you allow your subjective reality to dominate your daily life. It was developed as a mental discipline for those on their spiritual path who are seeking greater self-awareness, not as an escapist fantasy. So use it in moderation and consider your insights and your experiences objectively.

• The landscape you see reflects the current state of your inner world. Do not become preoccupied and fretful if you do not like what you see there; it will change as you become more self-aware. You must both have compassion for your failings and learn to master the wayward aspects of your personality if you are to realize your true self in the 'real world'.

• Although you may encounter archetypal figures in your explorations whose significance you will find described overleaf, your experience will be as unique as your dreams. Interpret them according to your own circumstances and trust your intuition to reveal their significance. Do not get hung up on the traditional interpretation.

• Record your impressions immediately after returning to waking consciousness and leave the analysis until you have recalled every possible detail. The full significance of what is revealed to you may not become apparent until a later date when all the pieces of a particular puzzle are in place.

• Accept that sometimes you will slide effortlessly into the meditation and on these occasions it may take on a life of its own, while on other occasions little may happen or you may even get stuck at one point in the inner journey. If this happens, do not give in to frustration. Come out of the meditation, do a simple relaxation breathing technique (see page 34), and leave it for another day.

• Be prepared to meet the personification of your negative attributes, or weaknesses, as well as your strengths and accept them as qualities in the making. Do not deny an aspect of yourself simply because it does not fit an image you like. Our demons are those aspects of ourselves that we deny. Face them as you would in a dream and they will lose their hold over you.

• Strengthen the connection with your guide over several weeks, or preferably months, before undertaking your first Pathworking exercise, and always ground yourself before embarking on each and every exploration of the inner worlds.

• Enter the inner worlds as did the heroes of mythology whose quests were, of course, analogies for the inner journey that we must all make in search of our true selves; that is, with humility, sincerity, purpose and a willingness to serve your 'Higher Self'.

THE TREE OF LIFE'S ARCHETYPAL IMAGES

The archetypal images associated with each sphere on the Tree of Life are as follows.

Malkhut (the Kingdom) – A young woman wearing a crown and seated on a throne.

Yesod (the Foundation) – A naked, muscular man.

Hod (Reverberation) – An androgynous figure.

Nezah (Eternity) – A beautiful young woman.

Tiferet (Beauty) – A young child.

Gevurah (Judgement) – A charioteer.

Hesed (Mercy) – A mature king on his throne.

Binah (Understanding) – An older woman.

Hokhmah (Wisdom) – A mature, bearded man.

Keter (the Crown) – An elderly king.

For a fuller explanation of the Kabbalah, consult other reference books.

PATHWORKING EXERCISE

Pathworking meditations are often highly structured and full of fine details to guide you through specific areas of the inner worlds. But if you feel confident to explore on your own the following exercise allows you to wander at will through the inner landscape, allowing images to appear spontaneously. If you do feel uncomfortable for any reason remember that you are always in control, that you can call upon your guide if need be, and that you can return to waking consciousness at any time simply by counting slowly down from ten to one.

Exercise: The two pillars

Get into your chosen position (see pages 30–31). Close your eyes, settle into a regular rhythm of breathing (see pages 34–35), and when you feel suitably relaxed, imagine that you are standing at the edge of a clearing in a forest.

Is it night or day? Is the sky clear or overcast? Is the air still or is there a storm approaching? Walk through the forest keeping your attention on the light from the sun or moon that is breaking through the clouds and flooding the clearing. Do not be distracted by any sights or sounds from the shadows.

When you enter the clearing you find yourself flanked by two massive stone pillars which are all that remains of an ancient temple, the temple of Malkhut. They symbolize the active male and passive female principles that govern and give structure to the forces of existence. When you stand between them you symbolize the middle pillar of equilibrium, and in so doing you can activate the energy that charges this sacred site.

Look down in front of you where you see a limpid pool which reflects the sun or moon framed by the pillars.

As you gaze into the pool you see the reflection of a figure on the far side of the pool. It is your guide. He or she is beckoning you to join them. Walk around the rim of the pool and follow them wherever they lead you.

When the journey ends thank your guide and gradually return to waking consciousness. Record your impressions straightaway in your journal so that you do not forget what you have seen.

the celestial court

Above: Tarot cards are thought to symbolize human archetypes and the various stages in the evolution of a human being – Wheel of Fortune (left) and The Fool (right). Although it is valid to use the cards as a stimulus for pathworking, the practical value of the tarot is as a focus for our intuition and insights into the psyche.

The following meditation is a more typical Pathworking exercise and a good example of how the technique can be used to explore and help balance the complementary aspects of the psyche. Do not be surprised if during the course of your journey your way is barred by one of the archetypal figures who may demand to know your purpose in travelling this particular path. You may answer as you see fit, or your guide may answer on your behalf. If you are refused entry at any point then accept that the time is not right to explore further and return the way you came.

Exercise: The Celestial Court

Begin with the Two Pillars exercise (see page 108), but instead of following your guide wherever he chooses to lead you this time you will wait for him to come to you. When you are face to face with your guide he will place his hands on your shoulders and you will lower your gaze.

When you raise your eyes again the temple of Malkhut will have been restored to its former glory and you will find yourself in the central chamber where the floor is comprised of black and white chequered squares symbolizing the complementary forces of the universe. Before you is the altar whose Holy of Holies is obscured from mortal eyes by a curtain embroidered with the symbols of the sun and moon.

Behind the altar are three doors each obscured by a drape upon which are depicted images from the tarot trumps. To your left is the Wheel of Fortune, symbol of karma; to your right is the Fool, representing free-will and self-determination, and between them the middle door is obscured by a drape depicting the card known as the World symbolizing discernment.

On this occasion your guide beckons you to follow him through the doorway to your left. Your guide draws the curtain aside and you step through into a cloistered corridor on each side of which you can see the novice monks and initiates of the temple as they were during life, reading, learning, worshipping and working in the grounds.

At the far end of the corridor you will come to the chapel of learning (corresponding to Hod on the Tree of Life, the sphere of the intellect). You enter and find a room whose walls are lined with books from floor to ceiling. Here has been amassed all the knowledge of the world, but even with such learning at their fingertips the monks knew that to acquire wisdom and understanding they had to go out into the world.

You pass through the library and into an enclosed corridor decorated with murals, paintings and tapestries depicting the history of conflict, the rise and fall of great empires and civilizations and the faces of the rulers and conquerors, now long dead.

At the far end of the corridor you enter the chamber of Gevurah (Judgement) which is empty save for a robed figure with an open book cradled in his arm. Your guide gestures you to remain silent as the robed figure details all the faults and failings that you have criticised yourself for in the past, all the hurtful things that you have done or said to others, whether deliberately or in error, and also those times when you have demonstrated a lack of compassion. No comment is made concerning your words or actions. These are simply statements of fact. What is your impression of the person you have been?

The book is closed and you are directed through a side door where you find yourself in a passage decorated with scenes depicting acts of charity, tolerance and compassion. Above the entrance to the next chamber at the end of the passage is a painting of a winged figure, Temperance, pouring water from one cup into the another.

You enter the chamber of Hesed (Mercy) where a second robed figure reads from a second Book of Life; this time it describes all your acts of consideration and kindness and the mitigating circumstances which are to be taken into account when considering your past mistakes. Again, no comment is made. These are simply statements of fact. What is your reaction?

Now return the way you came and when you find yourself back in the temple of Malkhut sit before the altar and consider what has been revealed to you. Consider that your present circumstances were created as a result of your past actions and that your future will be determined by your present thoughts, words and deeds.

When you are ready, thank your guide and gradually return to waking consciousness.

past life regression

Above and opposite: **Many people who explore what they believe to be impressions of a past life, are surprised both by the vividness of the imagery that they are able to recall and by how routine these lives seem to have been.**

'If you want to know your past life, look into your present condition; if you want to know your future life, look at your present actions.' (Padmasambhava)

Many people seek to recall memories of a past life in the hope of discovering that they have been a celebrated historical character. This is the way of the ego and it is fraught with difficulties for the ego is a master of self-deception. It can create a convincing collage of images drawn from memories of movies and books to satisfy our vanity, but these have a superficial reality and are quite distinct from the images that appear spontaneously in a properly conducted regression session. If you revisit a past life it should be for the purpose of greater self-awareness or to free yourself from a fear or phobia, not simply to satisfy your idle curiosity.

It is important to understand that this person from the past is not the 'you' that you are conscious of in waking life, but rather an aspect of your 'Higher Self'. That past personality is now integrated into the greater 'you', in the same way that you are a composite of your feelings. Sometimes you are animated by anger and at other times by love. You are more than the sum of your emotions just as you are more than the sum of your past experiences and incarnations. It is what you learnt from a past life that is important, not the mask that you once wore.

GOING BACK INTO THE PAST

It is a good idea to do this exercise in the presence of a friend, so that you have their support if you feel uncomfortable at any time. You should also record your impressions immediately afterwards to ensure that you do not forget anything.

Exercise: Journeying back in time

Get into your chosen position. Close your eyes, relax into a regular rhythm of breathing, and when you feel suitably relaxed visualize yourself standing at the top of a spiral staircase the bottom of which is obscured by clouds. Begin to walk down the steps and as you do so count down from ten to one very slowly.

Ten...your body is feeling heavy; 9...it is heavier and heavier; 8...you are feeling comfortably warm and relaxed; 7...you are sinking deeper into relaxation; 6...you are going down; 5...you are going further down, down, down; 4...your eyes are getting heavier; 3...you are fully relaxed; 2...you are going down to the bottom now; 1... you are completely relaxed.

Now pass through the clouds and into the warm, inviting darkness. You are in a tunnel. Ahead of you is a small sphere of light. Walk towards this light.

The light envelops you, and you emerge into a scene that is strangely familiar. Take in as many geographical details as possible. Is there a street sign or something to identify the location? Take your time and explore. Do you have any sense of the place or the period? What are your feelings about this location?

Look down at your feet and see what shoes you are wearing. Look down at your clothes, hold your arms out in front of you. Are you male or female? Young or old?

If you feel drawn to a particular building follow your instinct. Perhaps you will find a mirror there that will reveal more details. What are your feelings about the image that you have seen in the mirror? Are there any other people present and, if so, how do they react to you? Do you have any sense of their significance for you in this place and time?

If you wish, you can visit other phases of this life or other lifetimes by visualizing yourself entering another tunnel and walking towards the light at the far end. You will not have any conscious control over where you go, but trust that you are being guided to a place and time that has a significance for you.

When you wish to return count slowly down from ten to one, gradually open your eyes and become aware of the weight of your body and your surroundings. It is important to emerge from the semi-hypnotic state gradually and take time to recover your sense of the physical world.

As soon as you are 'centred' and properly awake write down everything you remember, but treat all your impressions objectively and, if possible, try to verify as many details as possible with factual research.

the power of
positive thinking

The book concludes with a look at
affirmations and the potential that they offer
for clearing negative conditioning, personal
transformation and for freeing ourselves from
bad habits. A 'meditation menu' offers a
directory of scenarios for clearing resentment,
cutting emotional ties, dealing with
disappointment, dispelling fear and worry,
coping with grief and loss, seeking guidance
from the 'Higher Self' and using colour
therapy in the context of a visualization.

affirmations

'Feel the fear and do it anyway.'

(Susan Jeffers)

No matter how self-aware, intelligent and unique we consider ourselves to be, it is a fact that we are all highly suggestible. Our choice of consumer goods is largely dictated by marketing people, our world view is influenced by the media and our moods can be manipulated by the comments and attitudes of other people – if we allow them. But we can free ourselves from negative influences, harmful mental habits and the effects of long-term conditioning by reprogramming our subconscious minds with positive suggestions, known as affirmations. These can be used as a mantra in meditation to create positive patterns and thought so that we can transform our perception of ourselves and of the outside world.

One of the best-known affirmations is the phrase 'Every day in every way I am becoming better and better,' which has become a cliché of the self-help school of psychotherapy. But the most effective phrases are those which you create for yourself in your own words for specific aims such as finding the right partner, becoming more patient or being open to new opportunities.

Affirmations can also reveal the subtle subconscious attitudes that prevent us from achieving what we want in life. When I first started working with the phrase 'Money flows to me in ever-increasing and abundant ways right now', I repeatedly stumbled over the words re-writing the line as 'Money flows through me', which revealed that I had a subconscious belief that it was not right for me to make money from something that I enjoyed and that it would always run through my fingers. Once I was aware of this attitude I was able to eliminate it by repeating the affirmation with a deliverate emphasis on the correct words to break down this conditioned resistance. I then watched in astonishment as well-paid work poured in after years of merely getting by.

CREATING YOUR OWN AFFIRMATIONS

Here are some guidelines for choosing your own affirmations.
• They should be short, simple, unambiguous and phrased to emphasize the positive. 'I have a fulfilling and well-paid job with time for myself in the evenings and at weekends' will create the right image in the subconscious, whereas 'I don't want to work long hours in a poorly paid job' will only reinforce your frustration.
• Always express affirmations in the present tense, as if what you want already exists. If you use the future tense you are implying that it might be conditional. You need to impress upon the subconscious that you expect your wish to be fulfilled.
• If you feel some resistance and you have checked that there is no ambiguity in the phrase you are using, persist, because if it is a long-term problem or attitude that you are trying to overcome it is likely that the ego will oppose it, just as it will have done when you first started to establish the habit of meditation.
• Reinforce the affirmation with a visualization on the same theme, but be careful that you do not sketch in too many details, otherwise you risk putting limitations on what is right for you.

POSITIVE AFFIRMATIONS TO USE

'I am on my true path and every day leads me nearer to my true place.'
'I am complete and perfectly acceptable as I am.'
'I live in an abundant Universe and there is plenty for everybody.'
'I enjoy perfect health and peace of mind.'
'I am fulfilling the purpose of my life which is becoming clearer to me each day.'
'I am calm and "centred".'
'I exist in the present, I let go of the past.'

meditations for different moods

Being on the spiritual path does not mean that you are immune to the frustrations of modern life. In fact, the further you go along the path the more your commitment is tested. Over the following six pages you will find meditations to help you to overcome specific problems. I have sketched a possible scenario and provided suggestions for suitable affirmations to use in each case, but as you become more confident and experienced you may want to devise your own visualizations based on the principles that I have outlined in this book. Whichever path you take, may it lead you to your true place and to a life of fulfilment and peace.

CLEARING RESENTMENT

If ever you feel that you have been criticised unfairly and have been denied the opportunity to tell your side of the story, or if you have been taken for granted, use this method to clear any leftover resentment. If you do not clear it, your frustration will eat away at you bringing more harm to you than the person you hold responsible for your unhappiness.

Exercise: Getting rid of an upset

Get into your chosen position. Close your eyes, breathe naturally and when you feel suitably relaxed imagine that you are sitting at a desk. In front of you are pen, paper, envelope, candle, matches and a bowl filled with water.

Look down at the blank paper in front of you and take up the pen. Now write a letter to the person who you believe has upset you, describing your feelings and explaining the situation as you understand it. It is necessary to express your feelings, as the primary

purpose of this exercise is to face and free your emotions. Once you have released your anger you will hopefully see the situation from a less impassioned perspective, and having done so you may now feel able to 'forgive and forget'.

When you have finished your letter imagine addressing the envelope (adding a description of the person if you do not know their name) and put the letter inside. Now ask your guide or 'Higher Self' to take it into the light. Visualize burning the envelope in the candle flame and when it has curled into ashes drop it into the bowl.

DEALING WITH DISAPPOINTMENT

To feel disappointment is to discover how badly you wanted something. Whether the object of your ambition is worthy of your efforts, and whether it is right for you is something that only honest reflection can reveal. If you are determined to achieve something, you can ensure success by visualizing yourself planning the necessary steps to acquire it, and then seeing yourself having attained it as a present reality.

'Difficulties and obstacles, if properly understood and used, can turn out to be an unexpected source of strength.'

(Sogyal Rinpoche)

Above: Expressing your emotions in the form of a letter and then burning the letter, can release surpressed resentment that might otherwise do you harm.

DISPELLING FEAR AND WORRY

Our imagination is the means through which we can create a new reality, but the thoughts and emotions which empower the process can be either negative or positive, so we have to be careful which variety we bring into being.

Although meditation should never be used to dwell on the negative, if you are at the mercy of fearful thoughts it can be useful to examine those fears in a visualization where you imagine the worst that could happen to you if your fears are realized. You might be surprised to discover that there is a limit to what can go wrong, and that it is not as bad as you had feared. Facing your fears head on in this way and naming them instead of allowing them to roam as vague, formless monsters in your nightmares should also be enough to strip them of their power over you.

COPING WITH GRIEF AND LOSS

Whether you have been recently bereaved or are grieving for the loss of something or someone that has meant a great deal to you, the following meditation should bring you comfort and peace of mind.

Exercise: Seeking emotional peace

Get into your chosen position. Close your eyes, breathe naturally and when you feel suitably relaxed recall the happy times that you enjoyed. Think of those times as a gift that has enriched your life and is now an integral part of your character. Such experiences can never be taken from you. Understand that death is merely a transition from life to life, that our divine essence cannot die and that what we are grieving for is our loss and not their passing.

Consider the parable of the grief-stricken mother who begged Buddha to restore her dead child to life and was told to find a house that had never known death. In the pain of grief we forget that no one is immune from suffering and loss. We all die and we all leave someone behind to mourn our passing. If there was no one to grieve that would mean that our life had touched no one and that would indeed be a cause for sorrow.

RELATIONSHIP PROBLEMS

It takes two to create difficulties in a relationship, so begin by altering your perception of the problem and 'centre' yourself so that you remain calm and objective in the midst of any upsets.

Exercise: Resolving difficulties

Get into your chosen position. Close your eyes, breathe naturally and when you feel suitably relaxed visualize the other person surrounded by white light which is the radiance of their spirit. Soften your heart centre by meditating on compassion. See the other person as a divine being whose human nature is as fallible as your own, but which is continually seeking perfection through experience.

Draw them towards you and embrace them while repeating the following affirmation: 'X and I are enjoying a good, positive relationship. Energy is flowing freely between us.' Then release them and watch as they fade into the distance.

If the relationship is right for you, the other person will sense a change in the atmosphere on a psychic level and should respond. Tension will be diffused and you will be able to talk matters through calmly.

CONNECTING WITH YOUR 'HIGHER SELF'

Choose or create an affirmation that relates to your present circumstances, or the specific question that you wish to have answered, and use it like a mantra to reveal the truth of the situation.

Exercise: Seeking guidance

Relax into a meditative state and say your chosen sentence or ask your question once. Then listen for an answer. Let thoughts rise spontaneously, but attach no importance to them until they cease to be random and meaningless. Repeat the affirmation or question a second time and listen again for a response. Repeat saying the affirmation for a total of 22 times, once a day, on 11 consecutive days.

Long before the final session you should find yourself holding a conversation with your 'Higher Self' which will be spontaneous, natural and flowing and will contain insights that you could not possibly have obtained from your conscious mind.

'Grief can be the garden of compassion. If you keep your heart open through everything; your pain can become your greatest ally in life's search for love and wisdom.' (Rumi)

You will know that this is a genuine communication rather than imagination because the words will flow faster than you can think of them.

TAKING CONTROL IN LIFE

Whether you want to free yourself from a bad habit such as smoking, go on a diet or be more in control of your emotions, the following exercise should prove beneficial.

Exercise: Practising self-control

Get into your chosen position. Close your eyes, breathe naturally and when you feel suitably relaxed identify precisely what it is that you want to achieve. Consider if anything is preventing you from achieving your goal.

Visualize yourself overcoming those obstacles. If you simply visualize yourself achieving your aim you will not be successful as your inner resistance will not have been addressed.

Gradually return to waking consciousness, note down any insights that you have received and act on them in anticipation of being successful. This will reinforce your resolve and make it easier to achieve your goal as you will not be struggling against inner resistance.

'Only in relationship can you know yourself,

not in abstraction and certainly not in

isolation.' (Krishnamurti)

Above: Writing an affirmation repeatedly on a daily basis can reveal the truth about a situation, breaking down any inner resistance or conditioning that might be preventing you from succeeding.

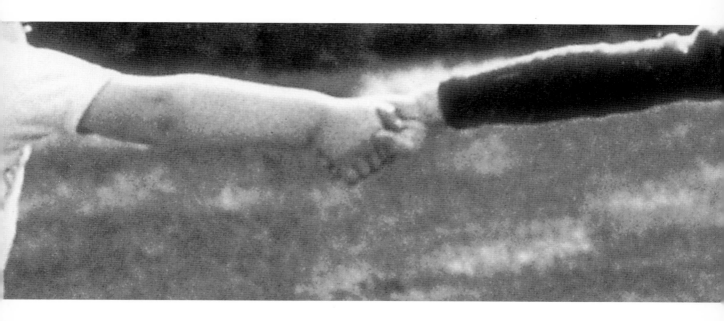

colour therapy

Above: Concentrating on a specific chakra
and its associated colour can stimulate
the appropriate physical and psychic
functions for healing and insight.

If you are experiencing any kind of problem worrying about it will only make matters worse. It focuses your mental energy inwards and can bring about fatigue and depression. Meditation expands the mind, alleviating the pressure and stimulating the release of endorphins – the body's natural painkillers.

If you lack energy or are suffering from a specific ailment you can visualize the colours that you need to stimulate the corresponding chakra (see pages 60–61). Imagine a sphere of coloured light and completely absorb yourself in it, or imagine being in a room in which the walls, floor and furnishings are of your chosen colour.

COLOURS AND WELLBEING

Different colours can also help with emotional and intellectual issues.

Brown is the colour associated with the earth and can be used if you feel you need to be more practical and more in control of your passions.

Red is the colour of physical energy, so is an ideal choice for those who feel lethargic or who are recuperating from a long illness. Red can also dissolve arthritic crystals, heal genital disorders and stimulate the circulation.

Orange is the colour that relates to emotions, so meditations using orange are often effective in dispelling anxiety, depression and stress-related disorders. Orange is also thought to improve digestion and heal disorders of the liver, pancreas and gall bladder.

Yellow represents the intellect and so is the colour to visualize if you need to make a difficult decision and you do not want to be confused by emotional issues. It is also good as an aid to study. It helps you to absorb more information, retain facts more effectively and recall them more readily. So meditate on the colour yellow before an important exam and you should experience less stress and achieve higher marks! Yellow is also traditionally identified with the regenerative power of the sun and is effective for healing on all levels – physical, emotional, mental and spiritual.

Green is the colour of nature and of harmony between the physical and spiritual realms. As such it is an effective calming colour useful for nervous complaints.

Blue is the traditional healing colour for all purely physical ailments, but it also corresponds to the throat chakra which means that blue is the colour to visualize if you need to communicate more effectively or stimulate your creative energies.

Purple is the colour associated with intuition and inspiration, so if you are looking for new ideas immerse yourself in purple and listen for that inner voice. This is also the colour to work with if you want to raise your level of psychic sensitivity or stimulate your imagination.

Violet is the colour you will need if you want to strengthen your resolve and help yourself through testing times.

White is the colour of purity and of the spiritual essence of us all, so meditating on white light puts you in touch with your spiritual guide and your own potential.

relationships – cutting the ties

The mind has often been likened to a restless baby monkey that does not take readily to training and, like the monkey, it is also a creature of habit. We tend to cling to thoughts that give us the illusion of security, even when it is obvious that the time has come to let go of the past or be pragmatic and flexible in the rules we live by and the standards we set ourselves. Reliving a failed relationship in your mind, reminiscing or indulging in recriminations and regrets do not alter the past, nor do they affect the person we may want to change. The only things they do successfully are drain our vital energies and postpone our future happiness.

Whether you are finding it difficult to free yourself from an emotionally draining relationship that has clearly run its course, or you are harbouring resentment from a past wrong (whether real or imagined), you owe it to yourself, and to the other party, to release the bonds that bind you together and instead channel your energies into creating your future. The following visualization will help you to achieve this.

Exercise: Letting go

Get into your chosen position (see pages 30–33). Close your eyes, and establish a regular breathing pattern (see pages 34–35). When you feel suitably relaxed, begin to visualize a small sphere of white light in the darkness directly in front of you. Watch as the light grows in size and intensity, radiating a warmth that you feel the need to surround yourself with and absorb, but which remains a short distance in front of you.

You begin to see a figure in the distance who you recognize as the person to whom you still feel emotionally bound. Observe them with detachment as they approach, for this is their spirit, their essence or true nature, and it shares the same source as you do. Whatever differences or misunderstandings may exist between you as personalities, in spirit you are brothers/sisters.

As you observe the other person understand that the essence of that personality wishes you well and that the problem that you perceive to exist between you originates with the ego, yours and theirs. Consider it to be a clash between the two individual wills which should instead be conforming to the 'Universal Will' that desires happiness and fulfilment for both of you; a happiness that you cannot even imagine at this moment because you are too self- or ego-centred.

Try to forgive that person of whatever wrong you feel has been done to you and in turn ask forgiveness from them for creating this disharmony between you. Do not be tempted to apportion blame.

Now begin to see the strands of glistening particles that have bound you in spirit to that person which you have created with your emotionally charged thoughts. They emerge from each of your chakras (see pages 60–61) and enter the other person at the corresponding chakra. To free yourself from the emotional attachment to this person, visualize them dematerializing or being severed at the source. If you want to, you can call upon any deity, spiritual figure or discarnate being such as an angel, your guide or 'Higher Self' to assist you. You can then ask this being or the 'Universal Life Force' to bless both of you and illuminate your true path so that you might both find your true place (and partner if applicable) in this life.

Affirm that you have no further demands on this

'When we forgive someone the knots are

untied and the past is released.'

(Reshad Feild)

person and that you wish them well in life. Then watch
as they return to the light and see the light dissolve.
When you feel ready, count down slowly from ten to one
and open your eyes. Remember, as you return to waking
consciousness, that the person who most often requires
your forgiveness, of course, is yourself.

index

acknowledgements

Picture acknowledgements in Source Order

Bridgeman Art Library London/ Private
Collection 110 left, 110 right
Corbis UK Ltd 20, 98
/Thomas Annan 113
/Dave Bartruff 107 left
/Michael Boys 94
/Jack Fields 15
/Earl & Nazima Kowall 17
/Kevin R. Morris 7, 100 Bottom
/Kevin R. Morrris 9
/Phil Schermeister 93
/Brian Vikander 100 Top
Octopus Publishing Group Ltd. 95 left
/Jerry Harpur 12 Top
/Peter Myers 6
/Bill Reavell 18, 19, 37
/Mark Winwood 1, 2, 3, 5, 10, 14, 22, 23, 25,
26 left, 26 Right, 26 Centre, 27, 28, 29, 30
left, 30 Right, 31 left, 31 Right, 32 left, 32
right, 33 Top, 33 left, 33 Centre Right, 33
Bottom Right, 34 left, 34 Right, 34 Top Centre
Right, 34 Centre, 34 Bottom Left, 34 Bottom
Right, 39, 40 left, 40 right, 41, 42 left, 42
right, 43, 44 Top, 44 Bottom, 45 right, 45 Top,
45 Bottom Left, 46 left, 46 right, 47 Top, 47
Bottom Left, 47 Bottom Right, 50, 52, 53 left,
54, 54, 57, 61, 70, 70, 77, 82, 84, 97, 102,
104 left, 115, 117, 119, 121 Top
Hulton Getty Picture Collection 12 Bottom Left,
12 Bottom Centre, 12 Bottom Right
Image Bank/China Tourism Press 96, 109
right
/Joe Devenney 65 Bottom, 66 Bottom Right
/Hidfki Fujii 68
/L Lambrecht 63
/G&M David de Lossy 81
/Tom Mareschal 64 Bottom, 66 Top Right, 125
/Carlos Navajas 48 left, 48 right
/Co Rentmeester 91
/Marc Romanelli 49 left, 69, 114, 116
/Guido A. Rossi 89
/Jeff Spielman 75, 92, 112

/Harald Sund 73
/G Tourdjman 80 Bottom, 121 Bottom
Leigh Jones 8, 51, 53 right, 65 Top, 66
Bottom Centre, 95 right, 109 left
Nasa 58 left, 58 right
Tony Stone Images/Jerry Alexander 99, 104
right
/Gary Braasch 67
/Peter Cade 49 right, 86, 87
/Ernst Haas 90
/Ernst Haas 122
/Karan Kapoor 80 Top
/D.C. Lowe 79
/Lisa Metzger 78
/Frank Oberle 64 Top, 66 Top Left
/Stuart Westmorland 88 right